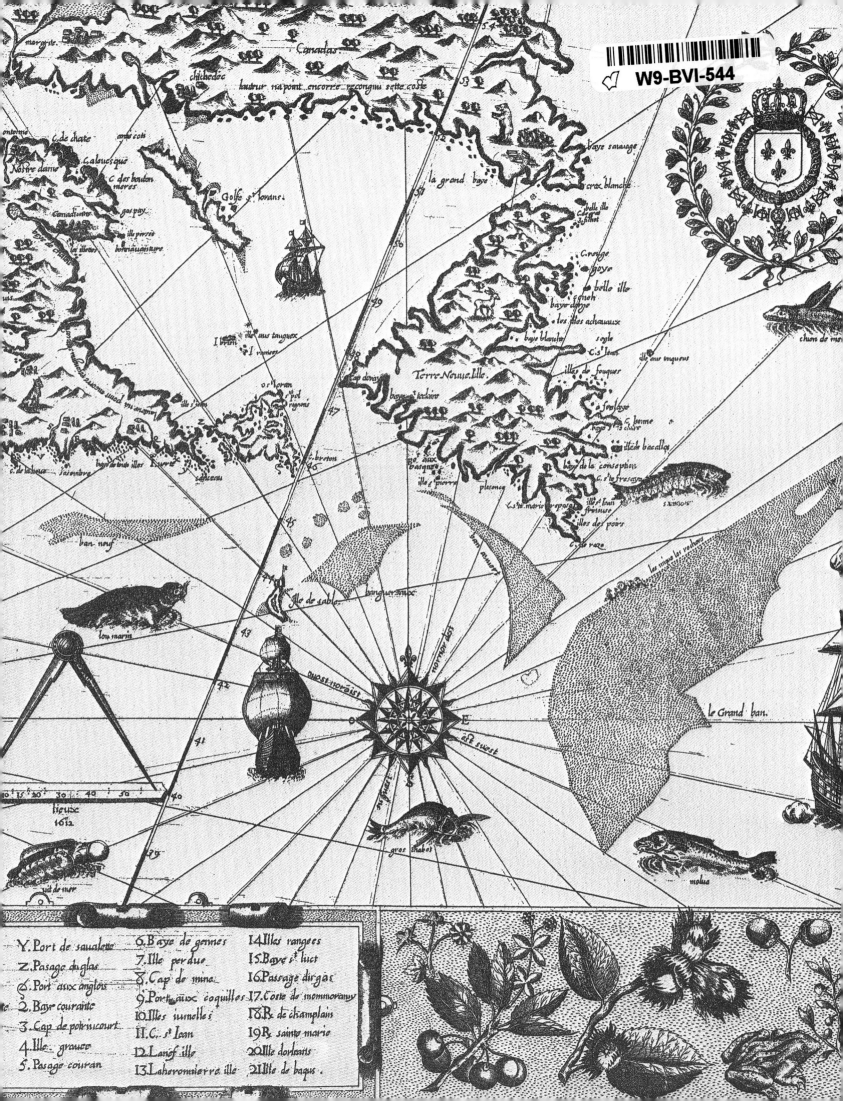

Canadas
chichedec

haubur na point encorre recongni sette coste

Golfe s. lovans.

la grand baye

Terre Neuue. Ille.

Ille de sable

banquereaux

le Grand ban.

ban neuf

lou marin

ouost norouist

E

aft suest

gros chabot

lieues
1612

molue

Y. Port de saualette
Z. Pasage duglas
Ꝃ. Port aux anglois
2. Baye courante
3. Cap de potenicourt
4. Ille grouee
5. Pasage couran
6. Baye de gennes
7. Ille perdue
8. Cap de mine
9. Port aux coquilles
10. Illes iumelles
11. C. s. Iean
12. Lanef ille
13. Laheromierre ille
14. Illes rangees
15. Baye s. luct
16. Passage dirgas
17. Coste de monmoransy
18. R. de champlain
19. R. sainte marie
20. Ille dorleans
21. Ille de bagus.

CANADA

CANADA

A CELEBRATION

Text by Robert Fulford

Photographs by John de Visser

Canadian Cataloguing in Publication Data
Fulford, Robert, 1932-
  Canada

ISBN 0-919493-12-2

1. Canada — Description and travel — 1950-
2. Canada — History.   I. De Visser, John, 1930-
II. Title.

FC75.F84   917.1   C83-098456-9
F1016.F84

Published by:
Key Porter Books,
59 Front Street East,
Toronto, Canada. M5E 1B3

Photo Credits
All photographs included in *Canada: A Celebration*
are by John de Visser with the exception of the following:
Fred Bruemmer: pages 191, 194 bottom
R. Cain: page 228 bottom
Ken Elliott: pages 36, 37, 82 top, 195, 214
Tim Fitzharris: pages 82 bottom, 177, 194 top
Imperial Oil Limited: page 34, 198 bottom
Zoe Lucas: page 41
Bob Mummery: page 175
Parks Canada: pages 38 bottom, 39
Roberto Portolese: pages 72, 113
Ken Straiton: pages 220, 222, 224, 225
Peter Thomas: page 228 top
Dudley Witney: pages 120 bottom, 121

Design by Gerry Takeuchi and Hannes Opitz
Editing and captions by Ken Lefolii

Printed and Bound in Italy

Page 2. Trail rider traverses rangeland in
Alberta. The Rocky Mountains loom above.

Pages 8/9. Bronze sculpture of an Iroquoian
Indian overlooks Ottawa's neo-Gothic skyline.

Pages 10/11. Annapolis Royal, Nova Scotia. A
French post established in the 1630s, it became
the most fought-over place in Canada, finally
falling to the British in 1710.

CONTENTS

60°　70°　80°

U.S.S.R.

ARCTIC OCEAN

ALASKA
(United States of America)

Beaufort Sea

50°

YUKON TERRITORY

Great Bear Lake

●WHITEHORSE

NORTHWEST TERRITO

●YELLOWKNIFE

Great Slave Lake

PACIFIC OCEAN

●Prince Rupert

Lake Athabaska

BRITISH COLUMBIA

ALBERTA

●Jasper

Vancouver Island

EDMONTON

●Kamloops

●Red Deer

SASKATCHEWAN

MANIT

40°

VICTORIA
●Vancouver

●Banff
Calgary

●Saskatoon

Lake Win

●Kelowna

●Lethbridge

Moose Jaw
●
●REGINA

Medicine Hat

WINNIP

CANADA

0　　　500km

UNITED STATES OF AMERICA

© SERVIZIO CARTOGRAFICO DEL TOURING CLUB ITALIANO, MILANO-1983-PRINTED IN ITALY

130°　120°　110°　100°

80°   70°   60°

GREENLAND
(Denmark)

Arctic Circle

CANADA

Tropic of Cancer

Equator

Tropic of Capricorn

Baffin Bay

50°

Labrador Sea

Hudson Bay

NEWFOUNDLAND

Labrador

James Bay

NEWFOUNDLAND   ●ST JOHN'S

QUEBEC

PRINCE
EDWARD
ISLAND   ● Sydney   40°

ONTARIO   Chicoutimi ●   NEW BRUNSWICK   ●CHARLOTTETOWN
                                                              Moncton ●   NOVA SCOTIA
                                          FREDERICTON ●
                         QUEBEC CITY ●   ●HALIFAX
                                                          Saint John ●
Thunder Bay   Trois-Rivieres ●
●   Sherbrooke ●
Lake Superior   Montreal ●

Sault-Ste-Marie   ATLANTIC OCEAN
●   OTTAWA ●

                                  ● Kingston
Lake Huron   Lake Ontario
TORONTO ●
Hamilton ●   ● Niagara Falls
London ●
Lake Michigan   Lake Erie
Windsor ●

90°   80°   70°   60°

INTRODUCTION

The armorial bearings of Canada. Heraldic devices are drawn from France, England, Ireland and Scotland.

Facing Page. Glacial meltwater cascades down Cougar Creek in the Rogers Pass area of British Columbia's Selkirk Mountain Range.

Canada can best be understood not as a nation-state in the traditional European sense but as a kind of empire. The twenty-four million people who live in Canada are as racially various as those of any great empire of history, and Canada governs territories on a truly imperial scale: some 9.9 million square kilometers, thirty-three times the area of Italy. Canada today resembles the Roman Empire in its late stages. A relatively weak centre (Ottawa) tries to control, over tenuous lines of communication and power, a series of very different, very distant, and increasingly fractious provinces, almost any one of which may abruptly declare that it refuses to accept the authority of the central power and demands independence. At a given moment two or three regions of Canada are involved in fierce economic-political disputes with each other or with the federal government, usually about control over some part of Canada's vast land mass—most recently, the rights to the oil beneath the land and the nearby oceans. Politically, Canadians are like the children of a rich man who made a faulty will:

their destiny is to quarrel forever, almost to the point of estrangement, over their bounteous inheritance.

To outsiders it may seem a peculiar fact of Canadian life that citizenship does not require adherence to the idea of Canada. A citizen in Alberta or Quebec or Newfoundland may openly declare himself in favour of withdrawing his province from Canada and yet still consider himself—and be considered by others—a perfectly good Canadian. In a sense it is as Canadian to oppose Ottawa as to support it. Many a Canadian politician has made his reputation by declaring, in effect, that he wants his province to remain part of Canada only *if* the federal government makes this or that concession. The art of a successful prime minister lies in his ability to find ingenious new stitches for old seams in the national garment of unity.

You can see this at its clearest in the words and symbols Canadians use to describe their country. People now of middle age grew up in what everyone called the "Dominion of Canada", the government at Ottawa was called the "Dominion government", and conferences between the regional leaders and the Ottawa government were called "Dominion-provincial conferences". But about fifteen years ago the word "Dominion" began to disappear. It was thought by many to connect Canada too closely with Britain, its "mother country" (another vanished term). So "federal", a quite neutral word, replaced "Dominion". Those same middle-aged Canadians grew up surrounded by symbols of royalty—there were crowns on the mail boxes and on the badges of soldiers, and *God Save the King* (later, *the Queen*) was sung at the beginning of each day in school and on many important occasions. But the crowns have disappeared, replaced by variations of the maple leaf flag which was adopted in the 1960s, and school children sing *O Canada* rather than *God Save the Queen*.

Queen Elizabeth II is still formally and constitutionally Queen of Canada, and all laws require royal assent from the Queen or her representatives, the governor-general in Ottawa and the lieutenant-governors in the ten provincial capitals. Royal assent is never withheld, and the will of parliament and the provincial legislatures prevails; Canada nevertheless remains a monarchy. The Queen and other members of the royal family still tour Canada and receive ritual homage, but these events lack the emotional importance they once possessed. Still, a visitor to Canada will notice more than a hint of royal connection in the nomenclature of the country. One province is called Prince Edward Island, a city is named Victoria after the longest-reigning British monarch, another province (Alberta) is named for Victoria's daughter, a famous dance company is called the Royal Winnipeg Ballet, Toronto has a Royal York Hotel and Montreal a Queen Elizabeth Hotel. These are lingering traces of a past that is now at last disappearing. In the 1980s no one would ever choose such a name for a new town or a new institution.

HARVEST DANCE.

A BURIAL.

A GAME OF LACROSSE.

BOW AND ARROW TRIAL.

WAR DANCE.

CANOE RACE.

THE PURSUIT.

TYPES, MANNERS AND SPORTS OF OUR INDIANS.

"Our Indians" appeared in the Canadian Illustrated News, 6 September 1879.

"An Encounter with Icebergs" appeared in Harper's Weekly, 12 June 1880.

These changes are among the visible signs of Canada's constantly altering view of itself. The reality of Canada changes with each generation, as waves of immigration transform our national life, but the way Canadians perceive themselves changes even more rapidly. The acquiescent colonists of the nineteenth century gave way—in imagination, at least—to twentieth century Canadians who began to see themselves as equal partners with the British in the Empire. There followed a bewildering (in retrospect) array of ideas about Canada's nature and destiny. The historian Ramsay Cook has noted that as the Act of Confederation that created Canada approached its fiftieth anniversary in 1917, "a Canadian historian ... explaining the meaning of Confederation might have concluded that his country's founders intended to build a nation capable of assisting Great Britain and her allies in their magnificent effort to make the world safe for democracy." That was seen as the highest purpose of nationhood, and it has since been argued that Canada in fact first achieved national stature on the battlefields of France. Ten years later it seemed obvious that Confederation had been created so as to lay the foundation for eventual Canadian autonomy. Ten more years, and it was argued that Confederation's purpose was to set in place a central government strong enough to deal with the calamitous economy of the 1930s. By the 1950s, another war having been fought, Canadians believed their role in the world was to help make peace, a belief that was buttressed when Lester B. Pearson, then external affairs minister and later prime minister, won the Nobel Peace Prize for his role in the Suez crisis of 1956. In the 1960s and 1970s many Canadians saw their national purpose focused on resisting American expansionism. In each era Canadians revise their self-image to suit the needs and opportunities of the moment.

The Canada of today—as distinct from the pre-historic Canada dotted with various Indian and Inuit civilizations—began life as a series of isolated colonies, and moved in slow stages toward a rough approximation of nationhood. There were short-lived Viking settlements in Newfoundland, the gigantic island province off the east coast of mainland Canada, as early as 1,000 A.D. The first more or less permanent European settlements took root there after 1583, when Newfoundland was first claimed for England by Sir Humphrey Gilbert, a great navigator and part-time pirate who, like many a sailor of his time, was searching for the northwest passage to Asia. Not long after, France was beginning the settlement of the shores of the St. Lawrence River and a few thousand traders, noblemen, priests, nuns, and soldiers were turning a small strip of what is now the province of Quebec into a distant branch of Louis XIV's French civilization.

New France lasted for more than a century and its memory still haunts the Canadian imagination. In a sense, it set a pattern from which Canadians of both languages and all races have since been trying to escape—the disruption of native life, the exploitation of Canada and Canadians by a distant and thoughtless power, and the imposition of alien customs and standards on a raw country. Among the native Indians the French made both allies and enemies; several Iroquoian tribes formed a war confederacy and relentlessly fought the French invaders. "They approach like foxes," wrote a Jesuit priest who had come from France, "fight like lions, and run away like birds." The French, from minor nobility in plumed hats to poor Norman peasants seeking a slightly less desperate life in a new place, felt that the Indians should be first suppressed and then converted to Christianity; for the most part they were successful only in the first of these goals. But New France turned into a rooted society that, transformed many times, endures and flourishes today, a unique bastion of French culture on a mainly English-speaking continent.

For a great many Canadians, and for all those who study history, the key date in our past is 1759, the year of the Conquest, an event still ruefully mourned in French Canada and still celebrated in parts of English Canada. On September 13, 1759, a British general, James Wolfe, with 5,000 men, ascended at night the banks of the St. Lawrence and drew the French forces under Louis Joseph de Montcalm into battle on an open plateau known as the Plains of Abraham. Wolfe and Montcalm both died in that battle, but the British forces won. This event laid the basis for everything, good and bad, that was to come in Canada. When the smoke cleared on the Plains of Abraham (now a park in Quebec City), the great age of exuberant French expansion in North America was finished and New France was transformed into a colony of Britain. As a direct result, all of Canada eventually became what English-speaking Canadians for many generations

"Indian Encampment on Lake Huron" was painted by Paul Kane, c. 1845.

"The Citadel of Quebec from Prescott Gate" appeared in the
Illustrated London News, 4 August 1860.

called—to the extreme annoyance of French-speaking
Canadians—"a British nation".

Under the British flag, Canada's many settlements—
established for fishing, farming, and fur trading—evolved toward
an eventual unification which to some seemed geographically
obvious, to others strategically necessary, and to still others
odiously oppressive. British-dominated governments were created
in the Atlantic provinces and in both Lower Canada (now
Quebec) and Upper Canada (now Ontario). All of them began
slowly to achieve the power to conduct their own affairs according to the British parliamentary model of "responsible government" in which the cabinet is responsible to parliament and the
members of parliament are responsible to the citizens.

By the standards of the nineteenth and twentieth centuries,
this process was exceptionally peaceful. There were minor rebellions which caused a certain distress to Queen Victoria's government back "home" in London—but democracy did not arrive, as it
did in the Thirteen Colonies to the south, in a single glorious

"North-West Mounted Police" appeared in Picturesque Canada, Vol. I, 1882.

moment. The achievement of freedom was a process of attrition, a gradual grinding down of Britain's colonial power. It took 172 years, the distance in time from the battle on the Plains of Abraham to the Statute of Westminster in 1931, when Britain acknowledged Canada's right to an independent foreign policy. Even after 1931, however, Canada remained a colony of Britain in one sense: its constitution was a British law, the British North America Act, and could be amended only by Her Majesty's Government in London. That remained true for another fifty-one years, until in 1982 Pierre Trudeau's government, after a series of arguments that lasted generations, finally (as Canadians say) "brought the constitution home." Today it can be amended by Canadians without reference to Britain.

In this long march toward democracy and formal independence, many of us see the roots of Canadian conservatism. The most important work of Canadian parliaments, legislatures and bureaucracies is conducted in a spirit of gradualism; and this, apparently, reflects the political temper of the people. Radicalism of left or right appears briefly here or there in Canada but never firmly establishes itself; every successful Canadian politician spends most of his career desperately searching for consensus. Political audacity is not often a part of our public life, and those who yearn for it are usually frustrated.

But a certain daring—a kind of nervous energy, married to grim determination—lies behind the expansion of Canada to the point at which it finds itself today. Canadian expansion was not, and is not, continuous and slow, like our political process. It moved ahead in leaps, from settlement to settlement, first in the Atlantic provinces and Quebec, later in Ontario, later in the West, currently in the Arctic. In many cases population moved because available land filled up: Ontario in the nineteenth century produced young men and women who wanted their own farms and could find them only by moving to what are now Manitoba, Saskatchewan, and Alberta. Eventually these population movements created what a geographer has called "The Canadian archipelago", a series of population islands set down in what is still, in much of the country, a wilderness. These islands of people are linked by increasingly elaborate networks of railroads, highways, aircraft routes, and telecommunications; but they remain islands. Crossing Canada by air at night, you see it as a series of separate, lonely spots of light and realize that isolation remains an essential part of the Canadian condition.

Turning this string of settlements into a nation was largely a nineteenth century accomplishment, and it was the nineteenth century that set the pattern of Canadian development and shaped the Canada of today. But before this could happen, Canada faced the last external military challenge to its sovereignty. In June, 1812, the same month Napoleon attacked Russia, the United States attacked Canada. The British, while conducting the war against Napoleon, had searched American ships and partially blockaded certain American ports. President James Madison's angry response was to move against the apparently vulnerable British colonies to the north. Eventually the war reached from the Atlantic provinces to southwestern Ontario; Montreal was attacked and part of what is now Toronto was burned. The British troops defending Canada also seized several settlements in the United States, and one expeditionary force briefly seized Washington. At the end of 1814 a peace treaty was signed, both sides returned their captured territory, and negotiations to establish a stable border were begun. Ever since, both the United States and Canada have claimed victory in the War of 1812.

One result of the war, in Canada, was a fresh sense of nationhood and a certain pride in military accomplishment. Another

"Interior of a Colonial Sleeping Car on the Canadian Pacific Railway" appeared in the
Illustrated London News, 15 December 1888.

was a renewed suspicion of American expansionism, a suspicion
which has not yet vanished though it has taken other forms. During the nineteenth century the fear that the United States might
eventually take over the entire continent was a spur to Canada's
own territorial ambitions. Canada turned itself into an empire
partly because it feared the growing empire to the south—and
feared it from a royalist, pro-British, anti-republican point of view.
This anxiety about American intentions quickened in the 1860s
as the Civil War made the United States, for the first time, a substantial military and industrial power.

Sir John A. Macdonald (1815–91), the first prime minister of
confederated Canada, was the key figure in Canada's response.
He symbolized the English-Canadian political view of his time.
He wanted a strong Canada, but he wanted it firmly within the
British Empire—he even suggested it be called "the Kingdom of
Canada", to tie it securely to the monarchy. Born in Glasgow,
brought to Canada as a child, he said: "I am a British subject, and
British born, and a British subject I hope to die." By making Canada stronger, he would also make it more British. In that mood, as
prime minister from 1867 to his death in 1891 (except for five
years in the 1870s) he—more than any other statesman—created
modern Canada.

The first of his achievements was the completion of Confederation to the Pacific. British Columbia, on the Pacific Coast, had
entered Confederation in 1871 on the understanding that a railroad would be built from the East to Vancouver. Macdonald made
good on that promise by shepherding the costly and difficult Canadian Pacific Railway through a long series of complicated and in
some cases corrupt arrangements that finally culminated in its
triumphant completion in 1885. This made it possible for Canadi-

ans to travel the breadth of their country without going into the United States and thus to develop independently of the Americans.

By thus focussing on communications as the hinge of nationhood, Macdonald was setting one of the patterns of Canadian thought. Ever since, Canadian public policy has been involved, to the point of obsession, with communications. The Canadian Broadcasting Corporation, with its two television and five radio networks, is the most discussed national institution of this century, as the railway was of the last, and Canadians have pioneered in the development of the telephone (invented by a Canadian), space satellites, and most recently videotex. It is no accident that the best known theorist of communications, Marshall McLuhan, was a Canadian.

Macdonald's second accomplishment, equally important to modern Canada, was his National Policy, a series of tariffs that protected Canadian manufacturers against foreign competition, particularly the competition of nearby American firms. That policy laid the foundation for Canadian industrial development; without it Canada would have developed as a much less populous nation emphasizing agriculture, fishing, and mining.

Macdonald's vigorous policies also contributed to the strains of Confederation. The national system he set in place left western farmers with a permanent grievance, which they feel to this day: they have to sell their wheat at (sometimes low) world prices, but they have to buy their manufactured goods from eastern corporations at (usually high) protected prices. Macdonald never understood the extent to which his policy enriched central Canada at the expense of the hinterland. Perhaps more important, he failed to deal sensitively with Louis Riel.

Louis Riel (1844-85) is a figure of great mythic power in Canadian history—the most famous Canadian opera bears his name and he's been the subject of television plays and radio programmes as well as biographies and novels. He was a volatile and charismatic Métis (the word means a mixture of French and Indian heritage) who led his people in two rebellions in the Canadian West, the first in 1869-70, the second in 1885. At various times in his life he was a schoolteacher, a member of the federal parliament (who was not allowed to take his seat), a U.S. citizen, an inmate of an insane asylum. In 1885, after a trial, he was hanged by the Canadian government, despite passionate attempts by the citizens of Quebec—his fellow French speakers and fellow Roman Catholics—to save him. Sir John A. is supposed to have said, "He shall hang, though every dog in Quebec bark in his favour." The execution helped make Conservatives permanently unpopular in Quebec; nearly a century later Quebec remains firmly in the hands of the Liberals.

The same can usually been said about Canada itself. Canada is not yet a one-party state, but for some decades the Conservatives who inherited Sir John A.'s party name have been far more often in opposition than in office; since 1935 they have directed the federal government for only six years. The modern federal government is largely a creation of the Liberals, and so is the policy that has dominated Canada's relationship with the United States, a policy of accommodation. With a few exceptions, the government of Canada has acquiesced in what is usually called "the Americanization of Canada". If Sir John A. was pro-British, the modern Liberals have usually be pro-American, and it is often said that Canada ceased being a British colony only to become an American one. American-owned companies do much of the manufacturing in Canada, and extract a large part of the resources of the country. American mass culture, in the form of television, films, recorded music, and publications, dominates Canada, even Quebec. Since 1967, the year of the Canadian centennial (an event celebrated at Montreal by Expo 67), there has been a persistent movement toward economic and cultural independence from the United States, and at times this movement has found expression in the federal government. For the most part, however, the United States remains the most important single fact of Canadian existence, a condition which its size and wealth probably make inevitable.

Canadians, in a sense, are themselves Americans, since they share so much of the American experience. But they are Americans who resist American ideology and American government; as the Canadians of Sir John A. Macdonald's time resisted republicanism, the Canadians of the 1980s resist encirclement by the threatening uniformity of American life and cherish their differences. They maintain, in world affairs and in their relations with the United States, a certain detachment. The Canadians live, by most standards, a pleasant existence. Enormous social tragedy is not, today, a condition of their lives. Their country has not been successfully invaded since 1759 and none of them has fought in a war, as a Canadian, since the police action in Korea ended in 1953. Nevertheless, Canadians bring to their present good fortune a melancholy past. Seen in rough outline, Canada is a nation populated by losers turned miraculously into winners. Our roots reach back to a series of defeats.

The French Canadians are the descendants of peasants left behind after the Conquest (the nobility went home to France). The Scotch came to Canada when they were thrown off their land in the Highland Clearances because the land could be used more profitably to graze the sheep of the rich. The Irish fled their country in the famines of the nineteenth century. The United Empire Loyalists, who settled much of central Canada in the late eighteenth and early nineteenth centuries, were the losing side in the American Revolution—the people who supported the British crown and thus found themselves unwelcome in the new republic. With each generation, the Canadian population is refreshed by

"Camp of the North-West Mounted Police at Rivière Courte" appeared in the
Canadian Illustrated News, 26 September 1874.

new infusions of immigrants—and in almost all cases they have
been displaced from their homes by tragedies of politics or economics. The last three decades brought Canada hundreds of
thousands of poor Italian peasants and similar numbers of refugees from the East European communist states. They in turn,
once firmly established here, found themselves sharing Canada
with still newer immigrants—from Pakistan and India, from the
West Indies, from Vietnam, from Latin America.

What possible form of government, what possible society, can
accommodate these people, and not only accommodate them temporarily as "guest workers" or exotic visitors but as full citizens?
At its best, Canadian society, with its talent for compromise born
out of geographical and historical necessity, can do it. Mythology,
a great American anthropologist has taught us, is "life-
supporting illusion." In Canada the great life-supporting illusion
is the dream of multi-culturalism, the idea of a "mosaic" of races
and cultures, living together in harmony yet retaining—each to
the extent to which it desires—its historic identity. This is the
essence of modern Canada, and on our best days it actually
works.

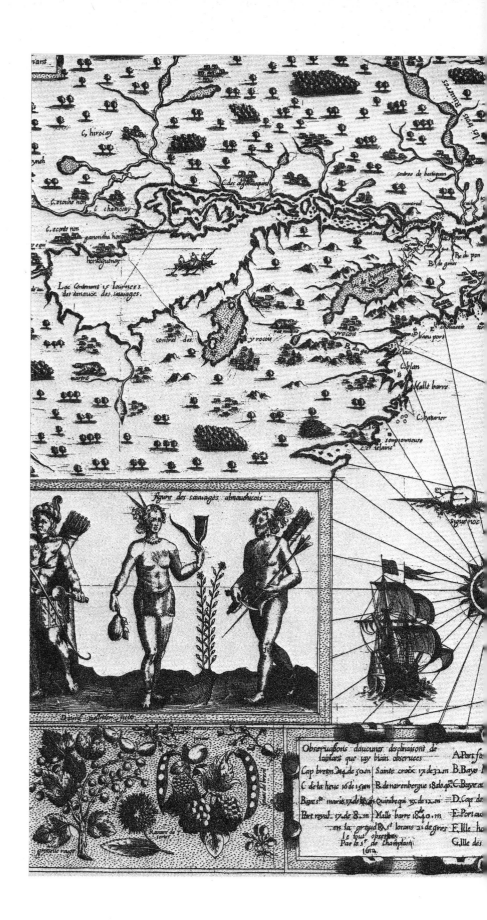

"Le Canada" appeared in 1653, but was based on a map drawn by the explorer and founding figure Samuel de Champlain in 1616. Several earlier maps had indicated the Great Lakes, but they were vaguely defined and based on hearsay. Champlain's map is the first to be based on direct observation.

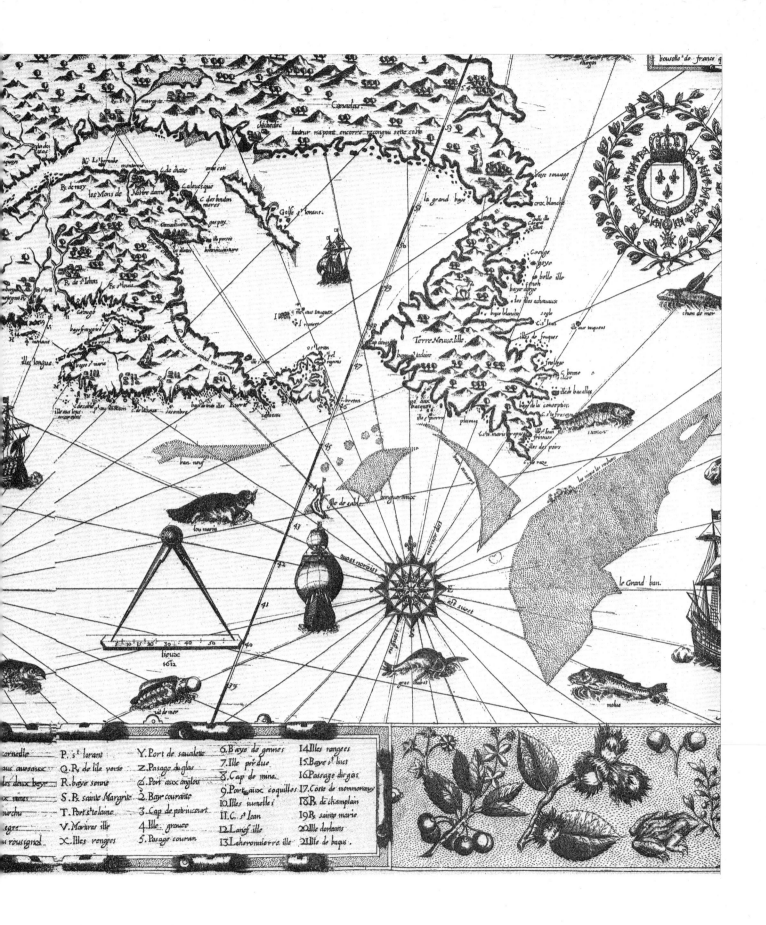

ATLANTIC REGION

NEWFOUNDLAND

NOVA SCOTIA

PRINCE EDWARD ISLAND

NEW BRUNSWICK

Atlantic Provinces

Newfoundland
Area: 370,486 sq. km.
Population: 567,681
Capital: St. John's

Prince Edward Island
Area: 5,656 sq. km.
Population: 122,506
Capital: Charlottetown

Nova Scotia
Area: 55,491 sq. km.
Population: 847,442
Capital: Halifax

New Brunswick
Area: 71,569 sq. km.
Population: 73,437
Capital: Saint John

Facing page. In 1921 the 39 metre fishing schooner *Bluenose* was launched in Nova Scotia. Last of her kind, she was five time winner of the International Fisherman's Trophy, and her likeness has appeared on Canadian ten cent pieces since 1936. A replica, *Bluenose II*, was built in 1963.

Approaching Canada from the East by sea, voyagers pass below the stone ramparts of the southern Newfoundland coast. François, a fishing village of 220 people, is one of the many hamlets known as outports.

Without roads or airfields, some outports are connected to the world beyond only by a weekly ferry that travels 400 km. to bring food, medicine and travellers to the isolated villages.

St. John's is the capital city and seat of government of Newfoundland. Many of the 154,820 residents still live in traditional, brightly painted clapboard houses overlooking the harbour. St. John's is a natural haven from Atlantic storms. Because of its strategic location, the port is a regular supply and service base for fishing fleets, offshore oil projects and Arctic expeditions.

Mile "0" of the Trans-Canada Highway: from St. John's, Newfoundland, the road runs 7821 km. through the provinces to end at Victoria, British Columbia. A modern, multiple lane roadway, it was officially opened in 1962.

Fly-casting for salmon on the Miramichi River, New Brunswick, a modern sportsman fishes a river celebrated by Basque and French fishermen in the 17th century.

Drying cod on Greenspond Island, a commercial fisherman does what was traditionally women's work. This operation is called "making fish".

Harvesting oysters with an ordinary garden rake, a Prince Edward Island man (*right*) gathers Canada's best-known variety of shellfish: Malpeque.

Cork floats (*right centre*) buoy up nets for seine fishermen. The nets catch cod, herring, mackerel, sardines and tuna.

Before either English or French settlement, Portuguese fishermen made yearly voyages to catch codfish on the Grand Banks off Newfoundland. Today hundreds of Portuguese fishermen, including those above in St. John's harbour, make the same voyage. Newfoundlanders named the Portuguese boats "the white fleet" after the color of their wooden hulls in the era of sail.

Wooden buoys (*left*) mark the location of lobster traps underwater. Newfoundland alone exports 45,000 kilos of lobster each year — by air to Europe.

Offshore, the seabed between Newfoundland and the mainland was once a vast forested plain, drowned by the ocean during an earlier geological era. Today, drilling crews are probing the seabed, outlining several oil pools that could make the region once again the source of great natural wealth.

Drilling platforms are part ship — since they must move from site to site on the ocean — and part artificial island. One such platform, the Ocean Ranger, went down in a hurricane-force gale. Many men died.

Right. Peggy's Cove, Nova Scotia, thought by many (including thousands of photographers, professional and amateur) to be the most picturesque seashore village in Canada. Here, the shoreline of the cove from the air.

Above. Atlantic breakers surge toward the lighthouse at Peggy's Cove, Nova Scotia.

Left. Herring gulls wheel above fishermen's stilt-legged houses on Grand Manan Island in the Bay of Fundy, New Brunswick. Fundy tides can rise and fall almost ten metres, the greatest tidal variation in the world.

Above. A superb example of colonial church architecture stands near Antigonish, Nova Scotia. From here the famous North Shore Drive winds forty kilometres along the ocean front to Cape George, the highest and most spectacular lookout point on the Atlantic coast.

Left. Acadian dancers at Digby, Nova Scotia. When the French settlers of the region, then called Acadia, refused to swear allegiance to the British in 1755, they were shipped south to the English colonies. This "dispersion" became the historic rallying point for Acadian nationalism.

The fortress of Louisbourg on the coast of Nova Scotia at Cape Breton was France's "impregnable" bastion in the New World. The stone walls were three metres thick and nine metres high, ringed with 148 cannon. Years after construction began in 1720, the cost had risen so high that Louis XV said he expected soon to see the towers of Louisbourg above the horizon of Paris. The British took it in 1758. Now partly reconstructed, the fortress has displays of weaponry, uniforms, and daily life during the French regime in the 18th century.

Magdalene Islands (*above left*) discovered by
Jacques Cartier in 1534, stretch for 100 km. in
the Gulf of St. Lawrence.

L.M. Montgomery made this house famous as
the home of her fictional heroine, Anne of
Green Gables. The building, now a museum,
stands in P.E.I. National Park.

Sable Island, 250 km. east of the Nova Scotia
shore, is home to a herd of 200 wild ponies. Grey
seals deliver their pups here in late January.

Built in 1899, this is the longest covered bridge
in the world. Its 391 metres span the Saint John
River at Hartland, New Brunswick. Covered
bridges had the advantage of protecting
timbers from bad weather, and shielding horses
from the frightening sight of white water.

Now a museum, the Carleton County Court-
house in Woodstock, New Brunswick, has been
restored to its 1883 look.

Hopewell Rocks (*facing page*) were carved from
the Fundy shores by wind, frost and tides.

ATLANTIC REGION

"British Troops on March Through New Brunswick" appeared in the Illustrated London News, 1862.

Canadian history, particularly modern Canadian history, looks different from the East. Where central Canada and the West see economic success and social progress (at least until very recently) the Atlantic provinces see disappointment, the repeated crushing of hope. With some notable exceptions, the onrushing development of twentieth century Canada has left the Atlantic region far behind, and the triumphantly expansive years in Ontario and most of the West—the years from the end of the Second World War to about 1980—were not a time of notable growth for Newfoundland and the Maritimes. True, the people became wealthier, because some of the prosperity of central Canada and the West spilled over, often in the form of federal government welfare payments and investment by Ottawa through the Department of Regional Economic Expansion. Canadians cherish the belief that each section of the country should be as prosperous as every other section (it's a kind of national religion, perhaps the only one we have), and many a federal bureaucrat spends his or her career tirelessly working out plans to make a poor region rich by the

Facing page. The Loyalist Burial Ground at Saint John, New Brunswick. British Loyalists fleeing the aftermath of the American Revolution founded Saint John in 1783. The oldest headstone here bears the date July 13, 1784.

Captured American frigate Chesapeake is led into Halifax harbour by the British battleship Shannon during the War of 1812.

clever application of hundreds of millions of dollars. But despite grants from Ottawa, despite dozens of optimistic programs for developing new forms of industry, the Atlantic provinces remain—in comparison to the provinces west of them—disadvantaged.

The "culture of poverty" is a phrase invented by sociologists a couple of decades ago to describe life lived at the margin; this is the life of the ordinary citizen in Newfoundland and the Maritimes. In Newfoundland a lobsterman, catching in wooden traps one of the most luxurious delicacies of the world's restaurants, may work a summer season of only a few months, at only reasonable pay, and then—lacking any other employment—spend the rest of the year living on unemployment insurance cheques from Ottawa. In Nova Scotia and New Brunswick, outside the cities, the lives of many farmers and fishermen tend to be focussed on simply making ends meet. Everywhere in the countryside are signs of what the textbooks call "occupational pluralism"—the man who repairs cars will also be a part-time farmer, the man who drives the school bus is also a part-time fisherman, the fellow who fixes appliances also keeps pigs. In some cases these are easygoing adjustments to rural life, and some of the people who make them are immigrants to the area, perhaps Americans who went there to escape the tension of life in the United States. Sometimes visitors to the Atlantic region—there is a heavy summer tourist trade in all four provinces—remark with envy on the relaxed attitudes of the local people. But, more often than not, those attitudes reflect a sense of deflected hopes, a melancholy realization that life will never be lived above the subsistence level. National television and national retail chain stores have made the Atlantic people aware of the riches which the rest of the country takes for granted, but the same central economy which produces the television and the chain stores has also arranged itself in such a way as to place those riches beyond the reach of the people who choose to live in Atlantic Canada. This has meant that over the years, hundreds of thousands of people have cast their vote on economic questions with their feet by moving across the U.S. border to nearby New England, or to central Canada, or in recent years to the Canadian West. At times the Maritimes' most notable export is brains, sent to staff the universities and the banks and the great corporations of the United States, central Canada, and occasionally Britain. This tendency goes back at least to the 1880s and has continued to the present moment.

What makes it especially hard to accept is the long and sometimes glorious history of the Atlantic provinces. This region is the part of Canada that first revealed itself to the astonished European explorers, fishermen and settlers—the French, the Portuguese, the British—and became the beginning of Europeanized civilization in North America. Newfoundland was populated by immigrants from the west of England in the seventeenth century, before Toronto existed. Nova Scotia and New Brunswick had flourishing local government and industry when Manitoba was mostly virgin grassland populated only by a few bands of roaming Indians and many thousands of buffalo. In the early nineteenth century Halifax was a notable Atlantic port and the vessels built in Nova Scotia sailed the trade routes of the world. There have been moments when the Atlantic provinces of Canada felt themselves at the centre of activity and looked to a future brilliant with promise. Today such moments still occur—most recently when offshore oil was discovered near Newfoundland— but they are rightly viewed with an inborn skepticism. There have been too many failures in the past.

Atlantic Canadians, their roots reaching deep into history, their ties to Britain much closer than most of Canada's, have developed over the years what seems to an outsider a deeper and more meditative approach to life. In their midst one senses life moving more slowly and deliberately. Elsewhere in Canada, in the last

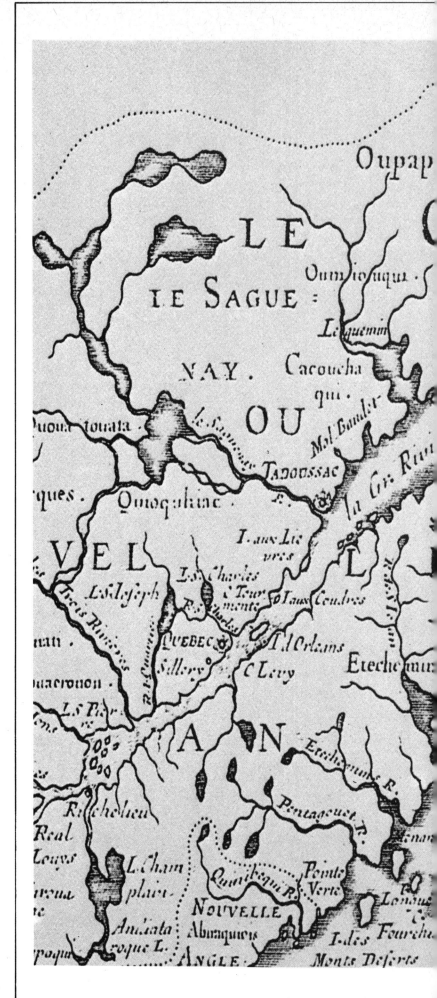

Overleaf. The Atlantic Region as it appeared
in a map of New France drawn by the first Royal
Cartographer, Nicolas Sanson, in 1656.

DE

Sauvage

Brest

Belle Isle

Port de Quartier

Cap de Grace

I. Fichet

Cap Rouge

Esqui= maus.

GOLFE DE

Gr. Baye

Baye d'Orge

C. Poinu

R. de Marimerate

Port de S. Nicolas

Port de S. Nicolas

Chicheslee dee

Port Neuf

ouet.

A =

rianites.

Canada ou de S. Laurens

ISLE

St Lau=

Bare de S. George

Baye blanche ou Claire

Anucosn, ou

Natiscosee, encor

Portens Purs

C. de lieres que

Culee Rossere

l'Assomphon.

DE

DA.

RENS.

TERRE NEUVE.

Bare de la Conception

C. de S.

Ste P.

papiguae

b.y Gaspe

des Metaes

Isle Plate

C. des Angul

Grand Golfe

I. aux Oyscaux

Bare des Trespalses

Cap de la Isles d'E

des Chaleurs

I. Ramée

des Chaleurs

Baye de Ste Claire

C. d'Ouest

I. Ste Croix

I. S. Pol

C. de Ray

ISt.

I. Brien

t. de Raye

I. S. Pierre

Iean.

I. la Madelaine

C. S. Laurens

Rembouteu

Cap Breton

C. Ensume

Omenamuel

S. Pierre

C. Breton

ACADIE.

I. Pelee

Seatori

Port Royal

Souricois.

C. Canceau

Passage de Canceau

NOU:

Paspay

Martengo

Maceme de

Bare de toutes Isles

la Heve

NOR

Isle de Sable

decade or so, the citizens, and particularly the intellectuals, have been involved in a search for "roots", for the historic background which gives meaning to contemporary life. In the Atlantic region this relationship comes much more naturally, because so many people can trace back their connection with their towns or villages for generations. In Toronto, and even more in Calgary, you are surrounded by what has just recently happened and by a sense of what is about to happen. In the Atlantic region—in a fishing village on the Avalon Peninsula of Newfoundland, in a potato farming community on Prince Edward Island, in a picturesque seaside settlement like Peggy's Cove, Nova Scotia—you are met with the lingering traces of what has been there in the past. The Atlantic provinces differ greatly from each other in dozens of ways, but this sense of history touches all of them as it touches no other part of Canada, and stamps them with a unique character. The Atlantic region is to Canada what the South is to the United States.

"This poor bald rock": that was the phrase once used by Newfoundland's most famous son, the pivotal figure in modern Newfoundland history, Premier J.R. (Joey) Smallwood, to describe his province. Newfoundland (which consists of the island at the south of the Gulf of St. Lawrence plus a large area of continental Canada, Labrador) in some ways is indeed poor. Its 404,519 sq. km. (nearly as vast as Sweden) are rocky and in a great many places inhospitable. When you drive across the island there are long lonely stretches that resemble the craters of the moon, and the little fishing villages (they are called "outports", though in fact some aren't very far out from the cities) usually back onto great forbidding hills of rock and look as if they might be swept into the sea at any moment. The fishing and lumbering on which Newfoundland has traditionally depended have been unstable and economically unpredictable. Newfoundland's fortunes have risen and fallen with commodity prices on world markets; even today its future seems to hinge on the vagaries of the oil market and the need (or lack of it) for the offshore oil under the continental shelf.

And yet this same meagre economy has been responsible for creating Newfoundland's special riches: its people and their sense of themselves, their sense of a special identity. Newfoundland in many ways is the most unusual province of Canada, and the way in which it is most remarkable is in the character of its people. In much of Canada the population is volatile and mobile, a constantly changing mix of strangers from around the world trying to turn themselves into neighbours and friends. In Newfoundland almost everyone is a neighbour to begin with. When two Newfoundlanders who aren't acquainted happen to meet, one may say to the other, "Who are you *one of*?"—meaning, which town or family do you belong to? Once that's established, to mutual satisfaction, the conversation can begin seriously, an intense exchange of reflections and memories based on a shared culture. For economic

"Will She Round the Point," a woodcut depicting Newfoundland fishermen, appeared in the Canadian Illustrated News, 16 September 1882.

reasons Newfoundland has not attracted any substantial group of immigrants since the nineteenth century. The people now there have been there for a very long time, the descendants of the west-country English fishermen who came in the seventeenth and eighteenth centuries and the Irish who arrived a little later. These two strains, mingled over the years, have produced a unique form of Newfoundland English—again, without parallel elsewhere in English Canada. It's hard to tell the difference in speech between, say, a resident of Winnipeg and a resident of Vancouver, but Newfoundland English is a unique, unmistakable argot. It carries the music of Irish-accented English but encompasses a vocabulary of words unknown anywhere else, including many that dropped out of use in England or Ireland a century ago. (There is now a *Dictionary of Newfoundland English*, a book of 10,000 words compiled by three learned professors at Memorial University in the provincial capital, St. John's.)

Michael Bliss, a Canadian historian, discussing the island's rather startling "racial and cultural homogeneity" has written:

"There He Is!" a woodcut depicting Prince Edward Island hunters, appeared in Picturesque Canada, Vol. II, 1882.

"The Newfoundland nation disappeared; the nationality survives intact." That word "nation" embodies a thousand grievances, for Newfoundland was indeed once an independent state (more or less), and its inclusion in Canada was seen by many Newfoundlanders as a defeat. Newfoundland was the last province to enter Canada, in 1949, and it did so only after lengthy soul-searching and bitter argument.

In the 1860s, when the other eastern colonies of British North America were being transformed into Canada, Newfoundland considered the idea and decided to go it alone. Between then and 1949 it moved erratically from colony to self-governing dominion, then back to colony, then to province. In the early 1930s it was the proud Dominion of Newfoundland, technically equivalent in status to Canada or Australia. But the Depression doomed its hopes of nationhood: ruined financially, rotted by corrupt administration, the young government had to surrender dominion status, throw itself on the mercy of the British, and revert to something even worse than colonial government—government by a body of commissioners appointed in England. That lasted until March 31, 1949, the day on which Newfoundland and Labrador officially became a province of Canada.

Many a middle-aged Newfoundlander can recall the black armbands of mourning worn that day by many citizens on the streets of St. John's. The argument over joining Canada had aroused contrary feelings—on the one hand, a sense of nervous pride in a separate identity that might be swallowed up in Confederation; on the other, a belief that economic progress could only come with a marriage to Canada. Joey Smallwood, a born orator, a master politician, a former labour organizer and radio announcer, led the Confederation side. He promised bountiful economic aid from Ottawa, which eventually came, and in a plebiscite his point of view narrowly prevailed, 78,323 to 71,334. Newfoundland, which began life as a kind of western extension of the European fishing trade, a stopping-place for sailors from Portugal and Britain and France, now became an eastern extension of North America.

Its life in Confederation has not been, by any means, entirely happy. Under Smallwood (who was premier from 1949 to 1972) the province searched earnestly and a bit desperately for the means to raise its standard of living. A Newfoundland historian, S.J.R. Noel, has written of an earlier day when Newfoundlanders were addicted to a "curious intoxicating myth which runs like a thread through history—that their land, underneath its harsh and unproductive exterior, is really a shining El Dorado, awaiting only the right leader to unlock its treasures." This myth continued to appear through the Smallwood era and after. An oil refinery, a wood products plant, a reorganization of the outport villages—each of these would help bring prosperity; each failed. In recent years, under Premier Brian Peckford, offshore oil has become the key. That remains, as El Dorado usually does, in the future.

But at the same time Newfoundlanders have discovered a new pride. In the 1970s, with a certain amount of gentle government prodding, their culture came alive again—in music, in the visual arts, in folk tales, in theatre—and a new generation of college-educated Newfoundlanders began to see the virtue in staying home on the bald rock rather than moving to the mainland for better jobs. They also rejected, en masse, the derogatory term "Newfie" and the Newfie jokes used by mainlanders—out of a misplaced sense of superiority—to scorn them. The rest of Canada acquired, slowly, a respect for Newfoundland. In a world where uniformity has become a curse, the inborn differences of Newfoundland came to seem more and more precious.

Every summer the 120,000 people who live on tiny Prince
Edward Island, near Nova Scotia and New Brunswick in the Gulf
of St. Lawrence—by far the smallest province in Canada, in both
population and geographic area—are joined by 600,000 to 700,000
visitors. Prince Edward Island in the summer, its white beaches
warmed by the Gulf Stream, is an idyllic vacation place. As a
Toronto publication said of the island, it's "a kind of dream never-
never land that most of us haven't known since childhood—
unsophisticated, slow-paced and satisfying." The tensions and
problems that burden modern civilization seem never to have
reached here. The island's largest city, Charlottetown, has 15,000
people and—outside the provincial government building, where
in 1864 delegates met to plan the confederation of Canada—a
daily five o'clock traffic jam that lasts between seven and eight
minutes. Americans from the northeastern States and central
Canadians make vacation homes here, sometimes buying abandoned farms. The Islanders, like Newfoundlanders, trace their lin-
eage back a long way; about a third of them are descendants of
Scots settlers who arrived in 1803. They fish the Atlantic around
them and grow potatoes in the bright red earth; for many years
P.E.I. liked to call itself "the garden of the Gulf."

The Island took its name in 1799 from Edward, Duke of Kent,
the father of Queen Victoria, and it was a writer of distinctly Vic-
torian outlook who gave P.E.I. its claim to a literary reputation—
a reputation which endures today in several corners of the world.
Among those hundreds of thousands of tourists who come every
summer there are always a few hundred camera-wearing Japanese who make their way immediately to the west side of Prince
Edward Island National Park, to a town called Cavendish. There
they photograph the Island's most famous shrine, a house called
Green Gables, the model for Anne Shirley's farm home in *Anne of
Green Gables* by Lucy Maud Montgomery (1876-1942), still a
favourite children's book in Japan and a dozen other countries.
Its story—developed in six sequels, in films and TV shows, and in
a perennially popular Canadian musical comedy—seems to
spring naturally from the soil of P.E.I. Anne Shirley is an inno-
cent rebel whose imagination, in response to the bucolic setting,
soars happily beyond the mundane world of her farming community. As she was when L.M. Montgomery created her in 1908,
Anne remains today: a perfect symbol of her native Island.

In Ernest Buckler's *The Mountain and the Valley* (1952), a
much admired novel set on a Nova Scotian farm, a man clearing
his land of rock can be heard to say: "That rock there is one my
father rolled out, and my son's sons will look at these rocks I am
rolling out today." That sentence summarizes what has come to
be regarded as a characteristic of Maritimes life, and particularly
of life in Nova Scotia—a devotion to the land combined with a
sense of family and ethnic continuity. In the novel, a lonely
man's relationship with nature helps reconcile his personal con-
flicts; nature is a character in the story, playing an animating role.

"Halifax, from the Citadel" appeared in Picturesque Canada, Vol. II, 1882.

That role may today be more nostalgic and sentimental than real, but it still exists as a lively part of Nova Scotian life and still informs the provincial imagination. Fishing, once primarily a way of life for independent men, is now often managed by corporations: the fish are brought in from the ocean by big, expensive trawlers. Farming has become specialized and commercialized by modern machinery. The people increasingly live in cities, such as Halifax and Amherst, and work at jobs not much different from the jobs they might find in Ontario. The need for capital has reduced the possibilities for an independent existence. Yet one can detect among Nova Scotians much more than a trace of the old Scots independence, and a proud sense of history. A visitor may well be reminded that among Canadian colonies Nova Scotia had the first newspaper (1752), the first printing press (1751), and the first university (1788). Nova Scotia's most famous son, Joseph Howe (1804–73), reform politician, civil libertarian, poet, pamphleteer, and great newspaperman, still symbolically walks the streets of Halifax, where he was born. His work is still discussed and reprinted. Only a few years ago a leading Nova Scotian writer, in an article for a national magazine, invoked Howe's early opposition to Confederation in arguing for a withdrawal of the Maritime provinces from Canada and their reorganization as a new state, Atlantica. The issues to which Howe devoted his political life (he was a late and reluctant convert to Confederation) are still alive.

"The Nova Scotian," wrote Thomas Chandler Haliburton (1796–1865) "is the gentleman known throughout America as Mr. Blue Nose, a *sobriquet* acquired from a superior potato of that name, for the good qualities of which he is never tired of talking, being anxious, like most men of small property, to exhibit to the best advantage the little he had." In the middle of the nineteenth century Haliburton was at once the celebrant and the acerbic critic of Nova Scotia and its people, and in those roles he became famous around the English-speaking world, his books being sold and quoted throughout North America and Britain. A convinced Tory, Haliburton put reformers, democrats, liars and braggarts in roughly the same category, and maintained a deep attachment to Britain (where in his last years he held a House of Commons seat). His reputation has long since retreated back to Canada, and particularly to Nova Scotia, where he is still revered for his original mixture of ideas, a mixture that at times amounted to crankiness. A lawyer and later a circuit court judge, he set down his view of human folly most successfully in *The Clock Maker: The Sayings and Doings of Sam Slick of Slickville* (1836), a series of dialogues between a traveller and his companion, a Yankee pedlar of clocks who speaks in homespun metaphors and similes ("Politics makes a man as crooked as a pack does a pedlar"). The term Blue Nose, which he applied to Nova Scotians, lasted to the middle of the twentieth century but has lately faded. Its most famous use since Haliburton's time was as the name of a schooner, *The Bluenose*, launched at Lunenburg, Nova Scotia, in 1921, which won international sailing races for two decades and became such a proud symbol of Canadian accomplishment that the boat's profile ended up on the back of the nation's ten-cent coins. A wonderful piece of work by any standards, *The Bluenose* was especially appealing to Nova Scotians because it revived lingering memories of past grandeur.

It was entirely typical that in the early 1960s, when the coal industry on Nova Scotia's Cape Breton Island sank into depression, the government turned for a make-work project not to some industrial development but to the history of Nova Scotia. Early in the eighteenth century, when France held Cape Breton under the name Ile-Royal, the French built a fortress town called Louisbourg. Captured by New England forces in 1745, it was returned to France in 1748, then retaken by the British in 1758. The British destroyed the fortification in 1760 as part of their conquest of North America. As a modern writer has put it, "The fortifications were exploded into timeless rubble. After a brief half-century of activity, the town's very site was left almost abandoned for generations." But then the interests of tourism, the make-work project,

Inside Fort Beauséjour, 1754, in the period immediately before the dispersal
of the Acadians.

and history came magnificently together. A small army of historians was recruited, thousands of original documents dealing with
Louisbourg were retrieved from France, and after a decade of
work the fortress rose again at enormous cost to the government.
Today a visitor to Cape Breton Island experiences a kind of time-
machine effect. The buildings are as they were, down to the last
detail, the attendants are dressed in the military and civilian cos-
tumes of the 1750s, and even the food a visitor eats is a replica of
eighteenth century food. Outside, the world rushes past on a highway but the Fortress of Louisbourg National Historic Park is
wrapped in a dream of the glorious past.

In 1980, in Paris, a Canadian won the Prix Goncourt, the most
important literary prize in the French-speaking world. On that
occasion Antonine Maillet made an extremely unusual remark.
"It is a prize accorded to a country and to the existence of a people," she said. "I have avenged my ancestors." Those were gran-
diloquent words, but symbolically quite true. Maillet, a professor
and a folklorist, a novelist and a dramatist, is French-speaking

and Canadian—but not, in the usual sense, French-Canadian. She is a member of a quite separate group, the Acadians, and is therefore the heiress to a tradition of displacement and loss. The book that won her the Goncourt, *Pelagie-la-Charette*, is an attempt to reassert her people's existence on the world stage.

The Acadians were French farmers, fishermen, and fur traders who began settling in what was then called Acadia (now New Brunswick, Nova Scotia, and Prince Edward Island) after 1605. For a century and a half this territory was bitterly contested between France and Britain, both of which rightly saw it as a gateway to the riches of the new continent. During the war of 1755–63, the British, doubting the loyalty of the French-speaking Acadians, decided to expel them. The Acadians were taken from their homes by British troops, packed into boats, and scattered among British colonies in America and the West Indies. A large number ended up in Louisiana, where a French-accented "Cajun" (Acadian) culture still exists. A remnant stayed home somehow, and others straggled back. *Pelagie-la-Charette* is an account of one group moving back home, overland from Georgia, in the 1770s. Until Maillet's triumph, the most famous account of the Acadians was embodied in Henry Wadsworth Longfellow's sentimental and popular narrative poem *Evangeline* (1847), which emphasizes the theme of homeless wandering.

The dykelands of Acadia. Raiders from New England repeatedly destroyed the dyke systems.

"Gorge below Grand Falls, St. John River" appeared in Picturesque Canada, Vol. II, 1882.

Today about four of ten residents of New Brunswick are French-speaking Acadians; in 1960, in an event politically symbolizing their full citizenship, they elected for the first time an Acadian premier of the province, Louis J. Robichaud. The land the Acadians held (some fled into the interior when King George II's troops came) or later reclaimed is marvelously various, and especially rich in timber—about eighty per cent of the province is wooded and lumbering is the chief industry. New Brunswick has never been so prosperous as when most of the ships of the world were made of wood and this area was (as a Canadian historian once described it) "England's woodlot". The Acadians now share the province with, among others, the descendants of thousands of United Empire Loyalists who flooded in after the American Revolution displaced them. Their influence can be most clearly seen in the small (24,000 population) city of Fredericton on the St. John River, which the Loyalists laid out in 1783 and which has been the capital since New Brunswick was made a province in 1785. There, among buildings from the late eighteenth and early nineteenth centuries, one realizes again that the Atlantic provinces are the part of Canada in which European civilization made its first permanent claim on the northern reaches of North America.

QUEBEC

JE ME SOUVIENS

Quebec
Area: 1,724,561 sq. km.
Population: 8,000,000
Capital: Quebec City

Facing Page. La Grande Hermine, a 24-metre square-rigger, was flagship on Jacques Cartier's second voyage to North America in 1535. This replica was built in 1966, using 16th century tools and methods, and is now on permanent display in Cartier-Brébeuf Historic Park.

Overleaf. Percé Rock was named for the opening, 18 metres high, 30 metres wide, that pierces one end of this island in the Gulf of St. Lawrence. Embedded in the pink and white layered limestone are millions of marine fossils. The island is now a sanctuary for gannets, cormorants, gulls and other Atlantic sea birds.

Early Québecois house on the rugged Gaspé Peninsula, south shore of the St. Lawrence.

Traditional St. Lawrence farms are narrow strips fronting the river. Only four percent of Quebec's land is under cultivation.

Right. Migrating snow geese stop at Cap Tourmente, near St. Joachim, every Spring and Fall on their way to and from Arctic breeding grounds. Once near extinction, the species now numbers nearly 100,000.

Previous page. Quebec City, founded by Samuel de Champlain in 1608, is the oldest continuously inhabited settlement in North America. When the fortress of Quebec fell to the British in 1759, New France fell with it. Today, eighty percent of Quebecers are still of French origin.

Above. Severe but beautiful, this Ursuline convent stands at Trois Rivières, Canada's second-oldest city after Quebec. There was a fur-trading outpost here as early as 1610; the permanent settlement came 25 years later.

Right. Joy-riding down the toboggan slide on Dufferin Terrace is a winter tradition in Quebec City. The toboggan is a distinctive Canadian design, borrowed by early settlers from the Indians of this region. The hotel in the background, the Château Frontenac, is also a Canadian design, borrowed from France, called in Canada the "railroad-chateau" style.

Canada's premier pre-Lenten festival, the
world-famous Quebec Winter Carnival, lifts the
spirits of the winter-weary for ten days every
February. The presiding figure, a giant snow-
man named Bonhomme Carnaval, looks down
on a dazzling procession of street dances and
float parades (*above*), creatures of the imagination sculpted in ice (*right*), hockey tournaments
and snowsport competitions, banquets and
balls, theatrical productions and musicals.

Notre Dame Cathedral in Montreal, Canada's largest church, accommodates 7000 worshippers. Built between 1823 and 1829, the building has two towers (named Temperance and Perseverance) that long dominated the skyline of Montreal. The superb stained glass windows behind the altar (*left*) are more than twelve metres high.

Although the Church no longer controls life in Quebec as it once did, more than eighty percent of the people remain Catholic. Rural roadsides are punctuated by small shrines *(right)*, and many of Quebec's cultural treasures are held by the churches: *(below)*, a fine early Québecois wood carving of St. Paul, and a silver madonna by Guillaume Loir, sent to Quebec by Louis XV.

Above. Canada's first true skyscraper, Place Ville Marie in Montreal, was completed in 1962. The cruciform tower rises 183 metres.

Right. Habitat, a residence built for Expo '67, was assembled from pre-cast concrete apartment units hoisted into place by crane.

Previous page. The façade of Montreal's City Hall, a fairly recent (1926) building, adopts the style known as French Renaissance.

Montreal's controversial sports stadium was designed by the French architect Roger Taillibert for the 1976 Olympic Games. After huge cost over-runs, work on the roof was suspended. An idle construction crane became part of the skyline, and the structure became the world's first partly domed stadium.

Quebec's fleur-de-lis flag, worn *(left)* by a young nationalist, was adopted in 1948.

Above. Quebec sportsmen race open boats across the ice-choked St. Lawrence. A similar competition was painted by the colonial artist Cornelius Kreighoff in the 19th century.

Left. Between Quebec and Montreal the St. Lawrence is spanned by several classic iron bridges. This one, the Laviolette Bridge, arcs three thousand metres to link Trois Rivières with Sainte-Angèle-de-Laval.

Above. The vast hinterland of Quebec remains inhabited mainly by wildlife. Here, fishermen seek salmon on a St. Lawrence tributary.

Right. Racoons are not only numerous in the wild, but adapt easily to urban environments.

Facing page. The most numerous species of bear, the black, is the only one that climbs.

Previous pages. 80: traditional Quebec farmhouse. 81: Beausecours Market in Montreal, the world's second largest French speaking city.

QUEBEC

"On The Road to Sillery" appeared in Picturesque Canada, Vol. I, 1882.

The great permanent theme of Quebec civilization, the theme which reappears in each generation in a different form, is *la survivance*, the survival of the French in North America. If Canada as a whole can be seen as historically aggressive, dedicated to the conquest of the northern part of the continent from Atlantic to Pacific, Quebec by contrast is essentially defensive. The Quebec people were left alone after the Conquest of 1759, an island of French speakers in the steadily widening sea of an English-speaking continent. Ever since, they have struggled to survive, and this struggle has shaped their politics, their economic life, their education system, their view of history—even their poetry and their songs.

Today the idea of survival is at the root of the debate over the future of Quebec. In the view of separatists, who want Quebec to become an independent country, separatism is the only course which will ensure the survival of French culture. In the view of federalists, who want to remain in the Canadian union, it is Can-

Facing page. Curving iron staircases were originally functional, doubling as fire escapes in a climate where searing fires were needed in the frigid winters. Today their graceful shape is a hallmark of Quebec.

ada which offers the best guarantee of survival because Canada will protect Quebec against absorption by the United States. All of Quebec political life hinges on this question, and in an important way national Canadian politics since the 1960s have been coloured by the same issue. Pierre Trudeau, who became prime minister of Canada in 1968, brought the question out of Quebec and placed it at the centre of Canadian public life. It has been there ever since, in one form or another, simultaneously a threat to the future of Canada and a promise of a more tolerant, more open federation.

For decades the people of Quebec have included a great many—and often these are among the best educated and most articulate—who believe their province must eventually separate from Canada. Whether they succeed or not, a separate identity already exists: in most of the ways that matter, Quebec has been for a long time a distinct nation with its own way of life. This extends far beyond language (though language is crucially important) into every corner of society. Traditionally, Quebec was Roman Catholic while most of Canada was Protestant, and in Quebec this meant that the Church played a significant role in everything from education to politics; for generations it used its power to maintain Quebec's separate existence by saving the people from the contamination of foreign (usually English Canadian or American) ways. Today the role of the church has diminished, but concern with Quebec's identity has not. Other forces have taken the church's place. Government, universities, schools, television, newspapers—they all play a part in stressing *la survivance.*

Since 1977, for example, Quebec has had strict laws governing the use of language in business. Every company, from insurance corporation to hamburger stand, must phrase its public signs in French, and businesses must show progress in "francization," the conversion from English to French as the language of work. There is a government bureau, the *Office de la Langue Française,* to enforce the law; its officials are sometimes called "language police." The English-speaking minority in Quebec has been allowed to maintain English schools for its own children but not to recruit European immigrants for them. English speakers who grew up in Quebec can send their children to school in English, but others must study in French. The government is determined that immigrants from Greece, Italy, the Caribbean and elsewhere will become part of the francophone majority and not swell the anglophone minority.

When these rules were introduced they were greeted with horror elsewhere in Canada and were called "rigid, dogmatic and authoritarian" by Quebec's leading newspaper, *Le Devoir.* Nevertheless, they quickly gathered support among the people of Quebec because they seemed a new and effective way of guaranteeing *la survivance.* The French of Quebec still feel insecure, still feel that

"Quebec," a steel engraving from an oil painting by L.R. O'Brien, appeared in
Picturesque Canada, Vol. 1, 1882.

their distinct existence is threatened, and many will support even
an arbitrary measure if it appears to lessen the chances of absorption by the surrounding English-speaking world. The Québécois
are a people endlessly searching for justice.

The English-French conflict gives an edge to Quebec life and
produces an undercurrent that is never far below the surface of
conversation or ordinary commercial exchange between members
of the two races. The English are seen by the French, with whatever justice, as beneficiaries of the Conquest, descendants of those
who took over the business and industry of the province in the
nineteenth century and treated the French with casual disdain.
For generations the English appeared to be rich, the French poor.
So today a French-Canadian, at whatever level of society,
approaches an English-speaking Canadian with an attitude that
includes at least some degree of historic resentment. The English,
for their part, tend to be nervous and defensive. They feel their
ancestors helped create modern industrial Quebec, and now they
find themselves unwelcome in the place where they were born.
Some tens of thousands have departed, usually for Ontario or the
West but occasionally for the United States. Those who stayed
have realized that coming to terms with the Québécois is one of
the major projects of their lives. Some do it happily, rightly regard-
ing Quebec civilization as vivid and exciting; others do it in a
mood of weary resignation.

Quebec's struggle touches almost every aspect of contemporary
life, from business school to popular music, from poetry to news-

"Quebec, A Glimpse from the Old City Wall," appeared in
Picturesque Canada, Vol. I, 1882.

paper writing. Each of these is different from its equivalents elsewhere in Canada. In English Canada, for example, business
school has no special social mission—it's a way to learn the craft
of management—but in Quebec a business school is a way of preparing French Canadians to assert the presence of their race in a
corporate world that has been dominated for generations by the
English. Popular music in English Canada is an adjunct of the
American recording industry, and Canadian stars are treated
with no special regard by their fellow citizens. In Quebec, however, a whole generation of *chansonniers* helped set the terms for
modern Quebec nationalism; one of them, Gilles Vigneault,
became the most beloved entertainer of his time and wrote a song
which turned into the anthem of Quebec patriotism. Poets in English Canada are much like poets elsewhere, their lives usually

circumscribed by literary magazines and university jobs. But poets in Quebec are part of the national struggle, and see themselves carrying the weight of Quebec's heritage on their shoulders. The very word québécois was first used in the 1950s by poets; later it was taken up by the *chansonniers* and finally by the politicians, until in the 1970s a new nationalist government came to power as the Parti Québécois. Newspaper writers, in the same way, are part of the struggle. In English Canada a newspaper writer is expected to be "objective," and to hide his politics if he has any. In Quebec, by contrast, newspaper writers are *engagé*. Everyone expects them to promote those ideas and causes which will further the grand cause of Quebec.

But perhaps the greatest of all the differences between Quebec and English Canada lies in their attitudes to history. English Canada is concerned with the present and the future; it maintains its naive belief in the future—a belief in a fresh start for everybody—largely by ignoring the past. English Canadians are less interested in the past than even Americans are. In 1976 the American Bicentennial was a loving celebration of history, but in 1967 the celebration of the Canadian Centennial was for the most part concentrated on planning for the future. English Canadians, as a general rule, like to forget the past; French Canada does not forget.

In Quebec, wrongs done long ago often spring to mind. In the First World War and the Second World War, for example, Quebec public opinion was against the military draft; conscription was imposed by the federal government and the (English) majority of Canadians. Quebec still feels those two events as violations of its rights, a double betrayal by English politicians. Today most English Canadians can barely remember "the conscription issue", but French Canadians speak of conscription in both wars as if these events happened last year. And they also speak—in newspaper articles, in TV interviews, even in private conversation—of Lord Durham, a man most English Canadians know only as a name in a high school textbook. To English Canadians he's a figure of historic interest, part of the long sequence of events leading up to parliamentary democracy. To French Canadians he is, preeminently, the man who prophesied the end of their race.

John George Lambton, first Earl of Durham (1792–1840), sometimes known as "Radical Jack", was sent to Canada by Queen Victoria's government after the 1837 rebellions. He spent five months in Canada and then, back in London, published his two-volume *Report on the Affairs of British North America*, which entered history as the Durham Report, a document that some English-Canadian textbooks call "masterly". Durham carefully separated those issues which required authority from England (foreign affairs and trade, to take two) and those which could be given over to the control of the colonies (for instance, schools). His report had a liberalizing effect on the history of Canada, but it

"Lacrosse on the Ice, on the Tank at Montreal," appeared in the
Canadian Illustrated News, 24 January 1880.

also sent a great chill of foreboding through Quebec. Durham
decided that the French Canadians had no future and did not
deserve one.

Cut off for eighty years from their mother country, cut off by
language from the rest of North America, they were—Durham
claimed—sinking into ignorance. "There can hardly be conceived
a nationality," he wrote, "more destitute of all that can invigorate
and elevate a people, than that which is exhibited by the descendants of the French in Lower Canada, owing to their retaining
their peculiar language and manners." What they thought of as
their most precious possession, language, was to Durham their
greatest handicap. He declared that the first object of policy for
Lower Canada (as Quebec was then called) must be its conversion
into an English province. He even believed, cheerfully, that intelli-
gent French Canadians would welcome their national extinction.
"I should be indeed surprised if the most reflecting part of the
French Canadians entertained at present any hope of continuing
to preserve their nationality."

Lord Durham's views did not prevail. As Quebec evolved within
Canada, French became the language of the legislature, the language of the courts, and the language of most schools. But Durham's views continued to hang over the future of the province,
both a threat and a spur to action. In the 1840s François-Xavier
Garneau (1809–1866) reacted to Durham's dismissal of French-
Canadian history by writing a three-volume account of Quebec's
past which described the courage, ingenuity and imagination of
those who had settled New France and explored North America.
In Garneau's hands, Quebec history took on a new dignity. He
became the first great French-Canadian historian, and part of his
greatness lay in his sense of purpose. He believed—and generations of later Quebec historians have since shared his belief—that

he could give meaning to the future by truthfully portraying the past. "I wish to imprint this nationality with a character which will make it respected by the future."

A layman, Garneau was seen by many Catholics as anti-clerical; parts of his work critical of the Church were suppressed. For Garneau, the survival of the Church and the survival of French Canada were not necessarily synonymous. But later in the nineteenth century, and well into the twentieth, the "ideology of survival" (as one historian has called it) became almost a Catholic monopoly. History came to be written in Catholic universities, usually by priests, and the protection of French Catholicism became as important as the protection of French-Canadian nationality. The two elements, in fact, were united in the work of the most important Quebec historian of the twentieth century, Abbé Lionel-Adolphe Groulx (1878–1967).

"Montreal Harbour" appeared in Picturesque Canada, Vol. I, 1882.

Groulx, a professor at the University of Montreal and a prolific author, provided the most potent intellectual fuel for French-Canadian nationalism over some four decades. He saw Quebec history as the struggle of French-Canadians to survive in the face of British determination to crush them. He popularized the slogan, *notre maître le passé* ("our master the past"), and he developed the idea of French Canadians as *une race élue*, a chosen race. He believed God was on the side of survival and the Quebec past was glorious because the people had remained faithful to both their religion and their nationality. He even spoke (in a way which makes those conscious of modern European history wince) of racial purity, the value of blood allegiance. "The future and Providence are going to work for us," he wrote. "God will not let perish that which he has conserved by so many miracles." He urged his students to pray for the coming of a great champion through whom French Canada could achieve its messianic destiny as leader of a triumphant French and Catholic culture in North America.

He was not an isolated or eccentric intellectual. Through his writing and teaching he imbued generations of French Canadians with a sense of mission. Today he may not be read as much as he once was; certainly he is not read in the same mood of pious self-righteousness in which he wrote. But there are few corners of Quebec culture which have not been touched by some secularized version of Groulx's philosophy.

The view of Quebec promoted by Groulx and other Roman Catholic thinkers was a success—too great a success, many modern Québécois would say. Separated from the secularized society of modern France by an ocean, separated from English Canada and the United States by language, Quebec not only survived but in a sense flourished. The population steadily increased, the language remained French, and under the Church's guidance the Quebec community achieved a tone of piety which made it unique in North America. Quebec developed its own version of Roman Catholicism, puritanical and conservative. The Church strengthened its control over education and resisted liberal reforms on the grounds that they contained the seeds of anti-clericalism. In general the Church tended to be comfortable with conservative politics, and unwilling to tolerate anything that might disturb the social order.

Federalism brought Quebec into touch with the rest of Canada, and Quebec even produced one of the great Canadian prime ministers, Sir Wilfred Laurier, who held office from 1896 to 1911. Laurier's political vision reached far beyond Quebec: he articulated a view of Canada's future which has not been equalled for ambitiousness by any Canadian statesman since. He said of the two founding nations of Canada, "We may not assimilate, we may not blend, but for all that we are still component parts of the same country." He imagined that Canada would soon hold sixty million

"From the Towers of Notre Dame," a view of downtown Montreal with Mount Royal in the background, appeared in Picturesque Canada, Vol. I, 1882.

people, he claimed that "Canada shall be the star towards which all men who love progress and freedom shall come," and he believed that "the twentieth century shall be the century of Canada and of Canadian development."

Meanwhile, inside Quebec, the two races were moving in quite different directions, each according to its cultural inclinations. The industrial revolution, accelerated by the First World War, was bringing factories to the cities and towns of Quebec and the children of farmers were leaving the land for better wages. The Church, secure in rural areas, regarded industry and urbanism with suspicion. Its educational system continued to emphasize the humanities and the professions—law, medicine, the clergy itself—and neglect commerce and engineering. Partly by default, but partly also because of superior financial backing from Ontario and the United States, the English minority in Quebec achieved overwhelming commercial dominance. Montreal became the financial capital of the new, industrialized Canada and the financial centre of Montreal, St. James Street, was an English and Scottish enclave. The French had survived, but

"Montreal, from the Mountain," which reverses the view on the previous page, appeared
in Picturesque Canada, Vol. I, 1882.

apparently they had survived only to be second-class citizens.
They controlled the provincial government at Quebec City, but
money spoke English.

Maurice Duplessis, who was premier of Quebec from 1936 to
1939 and from 1944 to 1959, saw nothing fundamentally wrong in
this arrangement. He cultivated the support of the conservative
clergy and the big English-speaking corporations, used provincial
police to put down labour agitation, and in general ran a government liberal critics sometimes described as 'fascist'. Duplessis
depicted himself as the champion of Quebec's rights, and even
when another French Canadian became prime minister of Canada (Louis St. Laurent held that position from 1948 to 1957),
Duplessis remained the passionate enemy of Ottawa. Through
the 1950s in Quebec the articulate opposition to Duplessis was
limited to a few intellectuals—among them Pierre Trudeau, a law
professor who was to be prime minister of Canada, and René
Lévesque, a TV broadcaster who was to be premier of Quebec.

Later the artists of Quebec played a lively and significant part
in the public life of the province, but in the Duplessis years they

were remarkably quiet. Culture under Duplessis tended to be *folk-lorique*, as the Québécois say: it emphasized the past and the simple virtue of the old *habitants*. An artist who addressed the issues of the moment, particularly an artist who criticized the clergy, was considered dangerous.

But in the middle of Duplessis' reign one small crack appeared in this blank facade, and perhaps that crack was the beginning of what later came to be called "the Quiet Revolution." On August 9, 1948, there arrived in a bookstore in Montreal a publication bearing the title *Refus Global* ("total rejection"). It was hardly a book, just a collection of loose mimeographed pages, incompetently typed, in a cardboard binder. Only four hundred copies were issued, but *Refus Global* turned out to be the most important statement ever made by an artist in Canada.

The author, Paul-Emile Borduas, was a forty-three-year-old teacher at the Ecole du Meuble in Montreal. An abstract painter, he influenced a generation of Quebec artists by importing into the province the French surrealism of André Breton and his followers. Like Breton, he saw the artist as a social goad and prophet. *Refus Global*, signed by fifteen other artists (among them Jean-Paul Riopelle, who would later become more famous than Borduas in both France and Canada), was nothing less than a call for the destruction of the Quebec social order. It contemptuously described the Quebec population thus: "A little people, huddled to the skirts of a priesthood viewed as sole trustee of faith, knowledge, truth and national wealth, shielded from the broader evolution of thought as too risky and dangerous, and educated misguidedly...in distortions of the facts of history." Borduas attacked the priests, the professionals, the established order, and "all conventions of society." He called for an end to theocracy and an opening to spontaneity and freedom.

From that point to the present, artists in Quebec have seen themselves as the vanguard of the new society. *Refus Global* was a challenge that injected new life into Quebec culture. But it ruined Borduas. He was attacked in the newspapers and a cabinet minister ordered that he be fired from his teaching job. Unable to find other work, he eventually left Quebec for the United States and later France. He died in Paris in 1960, the year that is generally taken to be the political beginning of the Quiet Revolution.

Maurice Duplessis died in 1959, his Union Nationale party began to fall apart, and the following year Jean Lesage and the Liberal Party took power. Among Lesage's cabinet ministers was René Lévesque. Under Lesage the government at Quebec City transformed itself and then transformed the province. The old rural image of Quebec quickly died and was forgotten with Duplessis. The Lesage ministers, and the civil servants they hired, were urban and sophisticated, the equals or betters of their equivalents at Ottawa. Lesage (and the increasingly powerful Lévesque) argued that the provincial government must take the lead in modernizing the province; now Quebec would have, for the first time, an activist government. Nationalization of the hydro-electric system was a major step. Later came a modern, secular education system, free at last of the clergy's restrictions. Above all, the Lesage government emphasized, the Quebec people would be masters in their own house. Inside the Canadian confederation, they would win from Ottawa enough economic power to shape their own destiny.

That became the central problem of Canadian politics in the 1960s, as the federal government of Lester B. Pearson maneuvered desperately to maintain the strength of Ottawa and at the same time allow for Quebec's ambitions. But the word "separatism" began to be heard increasingly. The terrorist *Front de Liberation de Québec* (FLQ), a loosely organized confederacy of separatists, tried to imitate national liberation struggles in such countries as Algeria and Cuba. The many FLQ bombings in the 1960s led eventually to the October Crisis of 1970, in which two kidnappings (one of which ended in murder) encouraged the federal government to suspend civil liberties. Meanwhile, other separatist factions pursued independence by legal and democratic means.

It was in the summer of 1967, as Canada celebrated the one-hundredth anniversary of Confederation, that René Lévesque finally emerged as separatism's champion. For years Lévesque

"Lumbermen's Camp" appeared in Picturesque Canada, Vol. I, 1882.

"Montreal: The St. Jean Baptiste Celebration, the Procession in St. James Street,"
appeared in the Canadian Illustrated News, 4 July 1874.

had sounded more and more like a separatist, but he was finally forced to reveal himself clearly by one of the most bizarre incidents in the history of the province—a provocative speech by the visiting president of France, Charles de Gaulle.

On July 24 de Gaulle was in Montreal to visit Expo, the beautiful and spectacularly successful world's fair that seemed to many Canadians the proof of their country's cultural maturity. In downtown Montreal de Gaulle spoke from the balcony of the City Hall. "*Vive le Canada!*" he declared. "*Vive le Québec!*" And then, after a brief pause, "*Vive le Québec libre!*" No one knew then, and no one knows now, whether he fully understood the meaning in Quebec of his words, understood that he was endorsing Quebec separatism. But intentionally or not, his speech was electrifying. As a journalist wrote later: "There was an immediate, explosive reaction from the people jammed into the plaza below the balcony. Separatist and federalist alike could hardly believe their ears. Neither could Prime Minister Pearson, who delivered such a severe rebuke on national television that night that de Gaulle cut short his visit and returned to France the next day."

After de Gaulle's plane took off, Daniel Johnson (who was by then premier of Quebec) remarked, "Well, de Gaulle is now up in the air, and so are we." Into a tense situation de Gaulle had thrown a grenade. The Quebec wing of the Liberal Party was placed in an exceptionally uncomfortable position. Pearson, the Liberal prime minister in Ottawa, denounced de Gaulle's remarks as an unacceptable intrusion into Canada's affairs, but the Quebec Liberals sensed that many of their own supporters applauded de Gaulle's sentiments and enjoyed the outrage of the English. In private the Quebec Liberals, among them René Lévesque, discussed their response, and that discussion led Lévesque to the conclusion that he must step out ahead of his party, must in fact go it alone. By the end of the centennial summer of 1967 he had issued a statement dismissing Confederation ("two nations in a single country...has had its day") and setting his course toward independence: "Quebec must become sovereign as soon as possible."

By November 16, 1976, René Lévesque was premier of Quebec, at the head of a Parti Québécois government pledged to achieve independence. But while his government proved popular, his vision of a separate state never captured the imagination of a majority of voters. He had come to power by placing the emphasis on good government (and the alleged corruption of his opponents, the Liberals, his former colleagues). In office, the PQ ministers discovered that, despite their advocacy, they could not bring the province to their side on the issue of independence. Gradually, in response to public opinion polls, they changed their approach: now they would promote a new idea, "sovereignty-association", an independent Quebec economically tied to the other nine provinces, retaining a common currency. Most of the English-speaking

"On the Beach at Percé" appeared in Picturesque Canada, Vol. II, 1882.

provinces, along with the federal government, rejected this plan. Nevertheless, in a 1980 referendum Lévesque asked the voters for the power to negotiate "a new agreement with the rest of Canada, based on the equality of nations"; he promised not to make this change without another referendum.

The 1980 referendum was the major political event of this generation in Quebec. The campaign between the *oui* and *non* sides ran for months and in many cases bitterly divided families. On May 20, 1980, Lévesque lost—59.5 per cent of Quebec's voters, including most of the 18.5 per cent who speak English (or some other language), voted against the proposition. At least for the moment the aspirations of the separatists were defeated and even the most passionately nationalistic Québécois admitted that for a good long time their province would remain within Confederation.

The struggle, however, was not over. In the early 1980s, and especially during the rewriting of the Canadian constitution in 1982, the Lévesque government continued to depict Quebec as the victim of Confederation, even though the federal prime minister and several of his most important cabinet ministers were French Canadian. At Ottawa, as any Canadian could see (and many Canadians resented), the French were in the ascendancy. But in Quebec not only the government but many of the newspapers and at least a working majority of the intellectuals believed that Quebec was still being cheated of its rights. In the first two-and-a-quarter centuries after the Conquest, almost everything about Quebec had changed; but something essential, something deep in the soul of the people, remained the same.

ONTARIO

VT INCEPIT   SIC PERMANET

FIDELIS

Ontario
Area: 1,245,970 sq. km.
Population: 9,000,000
Capital: Toronto

Facing page. The Southern Ontario peninsula was once covered by one of the world's great mixed forests. Each Fall rural and smalltown Ontario still blazes with the colours of changing foliage. This traditional galleried homestead is in Warkworth village.

Ottawa, the capital of Canada, stands on the Ontario shore of the Ottawa River. Queen Victoria chose the site in 1857. Goldwin Smith, the leading commentator of a somewhat later period, called Ottawa "a subarctic lumber village converted ... into a political cockpit." First built between 1859 and 1865 the Parliament Buildings burnt in 1916; they were subsequently rebuilt. The turreted form at the far left is the Château Laurier hotel. Many of the older cocks now crow in the Red Chamber, *below*, which houses the appointive Senate of Canada.

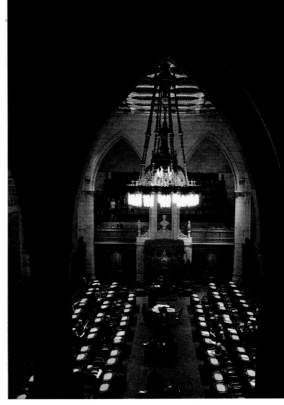

Overleaf. Costumed in the uniforms and firing the weapons of the War of 1812, modern soldiers recreate the battle formation known as a British square. The manoeuvre is part of a display at Fort Henry, which overlooks Kingston's harbour on Lake Ontario.

Previous page. Niagara Falls, with the *Maid of the Mist* bobbing below, continues to attract millions of visitors every year. Early estimates of the falls' height ranged up to a thousand metres; true measure: sixty.

Above. Downtown Toronto has been largely rebuilt in recent years, most of the new structures following the international style now common to nearly all the world's large cities. Here, the backdrop for the nineteenth century Flatiron Building is made up of several new glass-walled towers and the base of the CN Tower (*see pages 110/11*).

Facing page. Toronto has preserved some of its historic buildings by zoning law, some by public spending. The St. Lawrence Hall, an 1850s design in the Renaissance manner, served briefly as a legislative building but fell into disrepair until restored for cultural uses, among them rehearsals of the National Ballet.

Overleaf. The CN Tower, at 550 metres said to be the world's tallest free-standing structure, was completed in 1976 and is now the transmission centre for nearly all the city's radio and television stations. In summer, when the poured-concrete building material expands in the heat, the tower is calculated to rise five centimetres. Sight-seers can ride one of four elevators to the observation decks, or climb the world's longest staircase, 2570 steps. From here they can look down on everything worth seeing in Toronto except the striking new silhouette of the city created by the addition of the Tower itself.

Left. In the original Indian language of the region, *Tarantou* meant "meeting place." Toronto's present population of almost three million has been created by the meeting of people from every part of the world: among them Chinese (*top*), West Indians (*below*), Germans, Portuguese, Hungarians, Poles, and many others from Eastern Europe, the Mediterranean Basin and the Orient.

Above. Of all the cities within the city of Toronto, the largest is Little Italy. More than half a million Italians have helped transform Toronto into a cosmopolitan metropolis since World War II, and on the day of Italy's triumph in the 1982 World Cup soccer championship, many of them surged into the streets for a joyous, flag-waving celebration.

Overleaf. Ontario Place is a surprising, perhaps peculiarly Canadian, public institution, built by the Provincial government to give the people a Disneyland that has everything but fantasy. On or among three man-made islands with an area of 39 hectares in Lake Ontario are marinas and restaurants, a superbly original children's playground, a tented amphitheatre and a Cinesphere with a screen six stories high.

Facing page, above. Toronto's famous "clam-shell" city hall was designed by the Finnish architect, Viljo Revell, and completed in 1964. The design can be viewed as sculpture on a monumental scale, and it opened the way for the contemporary redevelopment of downtown Toronto. Adventurous projects since then have included (*far left*) a new concert hall, also in a sculpted shape but enclosed in glass rather than concrete, and a high-tech-styled shopping mall (*left*), the Eaton Centre, with more than 300 stores under a vaulted glass roof.

Right. Meanwhile, old-world traditions still flourish in the countryside near Toronto. A Mennonite family here returns from church in the carriage used, on these roads, through five generations of the same family.

Above. A few hours by car north of Toronto lies one of the great wilderness preserves of the continent. Algonquin Provincial Park covers over 7000 sq. km. and contains more than 2500 lakes. The park is a refuge for several species of wildlife, including game fish and the largest surviving population of timber wolves in the world.

Facing page. By far the greatest part of Ontario's land mass is composed of the Canadian Shield, the low pitted plateau left by the erosion of an ancient mountain system. This is the trackless terrain that made the famous Canadian bush plane — and the bush pilot who flew it — a necessity.

The Canadian Shield holds more fresh water than any region on earth, so that despite their lack of a seacoast, Ontarians turn to the water for recreation.

Summer resorts have sprung up throughout the Muskokas and Georgian Bay. Many preserve the old-world charm of the hotel at left. They offer vacationers cabins, cottages, canoes and sailboats, skiing in the winter and fishing in the summer. Game fish include the northern species, pike, pickerel, and muskelunge; brown, rainbow, brook and lake trout; and several members of the bass family, among them the courageous smallmouth.

Ontario's most celebrated water playground, the Muskoka Lakes region, attracts tens of thousands of vacationers in summer, is almost deserted in winter. Centreboard sailboats, like the Albacores racing above, have replaced canoes as the most popular sporting craft now in use on the lakes.

Above. Beside or on the white water of northern Ontario rivers are still often seen replicas of the birch-bark canoes used by the fur-traders to make the first voyages to the interior of North America. They took several months to journey from Montreal to Nipigon Bay (*below*) on the north shore of Lake Superior. Today, by the Trans-Canada Highway, the same trip takes two days by automobile.

Facing page. A special tourist train runs from Sault Ste. Marie to the head of the spectacular Agawa Canyon. The nine-hour round trip includes a two-hour stopover at Agawa Canyon Park. In winter a seasonal "snow train" runs to the canyon on weekends.

ONTARIO

"Muskoka Lake" appeared in Picturesque Canada, Vol. II, 1882.

Even this late in the twentieth century, you can sometimes hear a Canadian say of his ancestors, with pride, "They were from old Loyalist stock." That statement—as mysterious to some modern Canadians as to most foreigners, yet marvelously evocative to many others—hints at one of the central strains in the history of Canada, and the major theme of Ontario's development since the eighteenth century: the relationship with the United States.

"Loyalist" is shorthand for "United Empire Loyalist," the term given residents of the Thirteen Colonies on the eastern seaboard who chose, or were forced, to leave their homes after the revolutionary war and the Peace of Versailles in 1783 turned the American colonies into a new nation. United Empire Loyalists went to the established colonies in the Maritimes and Quebec, but the largest number went to Ontario, where they became the founding settlers. Everywhere they carried their hatred and resentment of revolution. Without them, Canada—and Ontario—would have been very different.

Facing page. Ontario has been shaped by influences from the United States, but there were times when American events were changed by Ontarians. One such time fell before the Civil War, when Josiah Henson, a slave from Kentucky, escaped to Canada. He helped establish the Underground Railroad, the route followed by later slaves escaping America, and in southern Ontario built this tulipwood cabin as a refuge for them. Henson was the model for Uncle Tom in Harriet Beecher Stowe's novel, *Uncle Tom's Cabin.*

"Kingston, from Barriefield" is in the John Ross Robertson Collection
at the Metropolitan Library, Toronto.

Today, if you cross the St. Clair River at Detroit and enter Ontario at Windsor, you may be more impressed by continuity than by change. The communities on either side of the border look much the same. You may see the same Holiday Inns and McDonald's hamburger restaurants, and you will find the people speaking the same kind of English. But in fact you have crossed from one civilization to another. Michigan and Ontario, both thickly populated industrial areas, spring from very different roots—the one revolutionary, the other anti-revolutionary.

Canadians have been defined as Americans who rejected the revolution, and certainly the mere existence of Canada is in a sense an anti-American statement, a denial of the expanding republicanism to the south. Canada, we can never forget, became a nation principally to resist the United States, and Canadian statecraft has been preoccupied over many generations with the need to assert Canadian independence. The major economic initiative of Sir John A. Macdonald's government in the late nineteenth century was the National Policy, a plan to protect Canadian manufacturers from American competition. The major economic initiative of Pierre Trudeau's government in the late twentieth century was the National Energy Policy, a plan to bring Canadian (rather than American) ownership to the oil and natural gas industry. The more things change, the more they are the same. All of Canada is touched by this history, and by the ambivalent feelings toward the United States that it leaves in its wake, but no province is more deeply affected than Ontario. The province of Ontario is the most Americanized part of Canada, yet it is also the centre of resistance to the United States.

This is in the Loyalist tradition, descended through some twenty decades of history, and shaped by that history. Some five thousand Loyalists moved to what is now Ontario. Like hundreds of thousands who came to the province after them, they were driven by the special energy of refugees, a mixture of desperation and hope. They helped to build Ontario's towns and industries, and to set the terms of its society. From the beginning, an aura of romance and heroism hung over them. Much later, Emily Lady Tennyson, the widow of England's poet laureate, Alfred Tennyson, expressed a common sentiment: "The United Empire Loyalists were a grand type of loyal, law-abiding, God-fearing men. No country ever had such founders." They were part of that sizable group (perhaps one third) of the colonists in New England who resisted the call to arms of the Continental Congress and in many cases joined with the British forces to fight the revolution. As a result, their lands were taken by the winners in the revolutionary war, and they were treated as pariahs.

In Canada, the grateful (and perhaps slightly guilty) British authorities gave them land, farm stock and farm implements. The British governor-general, Lord Dorchester, grandly declared that all immigrants who had declared themselves on the British side before 1783 should affix to their names the letters "U.E.," United Empire, in order to affirm "their great principle, the unity of the Empire." A kind of honour roll, known as the Old U.E. List, was officially drawn up, and for a long time after that—well into the twentieth century—there were many Canadians whose proudest boast was that they had an ancestor on that list. Later, after the Old U.E. List was compiled, others came in response to the British government's offer of free land. They were called, less impressively, "late Loyalists." They joined with the older immigrants in creating an agricultural economy in southern Ontario, at the western end of the St. Lawrence River system on which New France had been built.

These newcomers had declared their permanent allegiance to Britain, yet they were still in a sense Americans. They carried in their bones the early American experience of subduing the Indians and building a society far from their original homes (or their parents' homes) in Britain. They wanted to be part of the Empire, but as it turned out they wanted this on their own terms. They fought on the British side against the Americans in the war of 1812, but

"The Drive," a woodcut showing the annual drive of logs down-river to the mill-town following the spring break-up of the ice, appeared in Picturesque Canada, Vol. I, 1882.

they also were among those who pressed for responsible government and the development of some form of local democracy in the first half of the nineteenth century.

They were Yankees, but Yankees with a difference—and in a sense this is what the people of Ontario are still. Ontarians want American prosperity, American industry, American investment, American culture, but they also want their own government and their own identity. Having all of these things at once is difficult, and may in the end be impossible. Certainly it remains in our time, as it was a century ago, the main problem of Ontario life.

By the 1830s it was not yet seen as the society's central challenge. The American invasion of 1812 had been beaten back and the United States was still a minor force in the world. It was England's power, which could be asserted in even the minor details of life, that seemed oppressive to many Canadians. In Ontario as in Quebec, a revolution was being made.

In Toronto the main irritant was the ruling class, which drew its power through appointment from England. It was centered on a group that came to be known as the Family Compact, which met sometimes at the Grange (now part of the Art Gallery of Ontario). It was described by a historian as "A local oligarchy composed of men, some well-born, some ill-born, some brilliant, some stupid, whom the caprices of a small provincial society, with a code all its own, had pitchforked into power." It was this Family Compact—conservative, royalist, protective of its own interests—that William Lyon Mackenzie saw as his, and his society's, enemy.

Mackenzie (1795–1861) is that rarity in history, an unsuccessful revolutionary who nevertheless lived a long life and ended up a hero to his fellow citizens. Today his house in Toronto is one of the city's few historic shrines and the history books regard him benignly as a founder of Canadian democracy.

In his lifetime he was a much more controversial figure, a popular politician and journalist who aroused hatred as well as admiration. Born in Scotland, he came to Canada at the age of twenty-five. Four years later he was publishing a newspaper, the *Colonial Advocate*, which attacked the rulers of the colony; four years after that he was elected to the Legislative Assembly of Upper Canada, the predecessor of today's Ontario legislature; seven years after that he was the first mayor of Toronto; and two years later, in December, 1837, he was inciting the closest thing to a revolution that Ontario has ever seen.

His actions often suggested mental instability, and more than one historian has concluded that during the rebellion his mind

"The Battle of Lake Champlain," depicting a naval encounter during the War of 1812, is from an oil painting by Chappel.

was unbalanced. But he mustered a small body of troops and set out to bring down the government. There was one minor skirmish on the northern fringes of Toronto; then Mackenzie fled to the United States and his men dispersed. For a time, on Navy Island, north of Niagara Falls, he claimed to have established an independent republic—a typically eccentric gesture. Eventually the Americans imprisoned him for violating their neutrality laws, and when he emerged he became an American journalist, turning out anti-British tracts. An act of amnesty allowed him to return to Canada, where he returned to politics and journalism. Sixty years after his death, his grandson, William Lyon Mackenzie King (1874–1950), became prime minister of Canada.

It was in Mackenzie's time that Toronto changed from the trading centre of a small rural economy into a capital city—first the capital of the old Province of Upper Canada, then the capital of the province of Ontario. Today it contains not only the financial power of Canada as a whole (which it drew away from Montreal about half a century ago) but the cultural leadership of English Canada—the television networks, the book publishing houses, the national magazines, the most influential universities, a national newspaper. Much despised and envied by Canadians elsewhere (once it was popularly known as "Hog Town"), it has nevertheless made itself the centre. And today, as Canada faces the unavoidable question of American power, Toronto is the focus for both sides of the debate—between the multi-national corporations (whose Canadian branch plants have head offices in Toronto) and the most passionate opponents of Americanization (who can usually be found in the universities and the media).

"Toronto, from the Island" appeared in Picturesque Canada, Vol. I, 1882.

"A Sculling Match, Toronto Harbour" appeared in Picturesque Canada, Vol. 1, 1882.

The rebels of Mackenzie's generation drew some of their spiritual strength from the example of the Americans, and Mackenzie's use of the United States as a sanctuary reinforced the view that an alternative form of government was at hand. Partly because of Mackenzie's rebellion, but also because of widespread discontent, the British slowly liberalized their control of their Canadian colonies. By the time of Confederation, in 1867, Canada was beginning to function as a democracy. Now Britain was no longer an absentee dictatorship: it was seen as a benign force and even a protector. Canadian independence was threatened not from London but from the United States. This threat seemed all the more real in the 1860s when a group of Irish-American rebels, the Fenians, unsuccessfully tried to invade Canada and set up a new republic.

Pro-British sentiment soon dominated Ontario. Where else, the people of Ontario asked, could they look for help? In the 1870s there were four million Canadians as against forty million Americans, and the U.S was now (after the Civil War) a military as well as an industrial power. For the next half-century, Ontario and

"Whitby Races, The Queen's Plate" depicting a thoroughbred race that has been run every year since that time, appeared in the Canadian Illustrated News, 11 June 1870.

every aspect of Ontario life, from trade unionism to education, had a British coloration. When feminism appeared in Ontario, its inspiration was British feminism; so with socialism and, to an important extent, religion. Britain was the chief source of immigration to Ontario and the chief market for Canada's raw materials. It was the source, too, for capital financing, and Canadian businessmen looked to Britain for leadership.

The people of Ontario (unlike the people of Quebec) came to a new understanding of their future; they would be independent, but independently British. In the population as a whole this took the form of faithful adherence to Queen Victoria, a great deal of Union Jack-waving, and later an almost hysterical eagerness to join Britain in the 1914–18 war. Among intellectuals in Ontario, there was a more sophisticated but similar view. The imperial connection with London would extend Canada's role in the world, the intellectuals came to believe. They became passionately pro-British, passionately anti-American. Oxford and Cambridge were seen as the summit of intellectual achievement, and the typical Canadian intellectual was often a kind of imitation Englishman. In Ottawa the civil service was organized largely on British lines by an elite group largely trained in Britain.

In the years between the First World War and the Second, this adherence to Britain gradually lost its strength and became increasingly separated from reality. Ontario still saw itself as "British," but trade was shifting to the United States, and a continental economy was being organized from America. The great lumber and mining companies found their markets not in England but closer to hand in the United States; sometimes they came under American ownership. At the beginning of the great age of the automobile, there were Canadian car manufacturers, producing cars to their own designs. When the auto industry was rationalized the Canadians sold out not to the British but to the emerging giants of Detroit, notably General Motors. In trade, the Anglo-Canadian alliance was slowly collapsing.

In its own politics, Ontario was developing a system that made it unique in Canada and very exceptional among democracies in the world — a kind of elected one-party government, with a permanently frustrated opposition. From 1943 to the present, Ontario has been governed by the Progressive Conservative Party; most citizens have known no other kind of provincial government. Under four premiers, through majority government and minority government, against the most passionate challenges of two generations of opposition politicians, the Conservatives have held onto power. One reason is that the opposition has always been divided and has shown no signs of uniting: the Liberals and socialists dislike each other more than either dislikes the Conservatives. For their part the Conservatives have been exceptionally adroit politicians. Their leadership has shown a certain demographic consistency — each premier has been a male Anglo-Saxon Protestant lawyer from a small city — but the policies have changed at least as often as the premiers. The Conservatives have been more than ready to adapt to each shift in the views of the voters. When Ontario people wanted a non-interventionist government, holding high the banner of free enterprise, the Conservatives provided it. Later, when Ontario wanted a more active government, playing a large role in the economy and culture as well as in such traditional provincial realms as education and highways, the Conservatives proved they could provide that, too. The Conservatives are flexible political managers who can change their outlook on almost any question without ever appearing to betray their past.

In recent years they have been trying to adapt to what public rhetoric calls "multi-culturalism" and political bosses call, more prosaically, "the ethnic vote." For more than a generation the Conservatives held power on the basis of rural and small-town voters, most of them the descendants of British immigrants. Slowly the population has changed, so that many areas are now dominated by fairly recent Italian, Greek and East European immigrants and more recent immigrants from Portugal, the West Indies, and Asia. Among other things, the immigrants have changed the religious character of the province's biggest city.

Toronto, a Protestant stronghold for more than a century, now has more Roman Catholics than Protestants. These voters are not by instinct Conservative, and many of them have developed allegiances to the Liberals and the socialist New Democrats. As they achieve citizenship and take part in politics, they constitute a growing threat to Conservative hegemony.

They also constitute the most interesting development in the life of Ontario in the second half of this century. Their presence and their influence are facts of life that young people take for granted but the middle-aged sometimes regard with astonishment. A fifty-year-old who has lived in Ontario since the 1930s has seen it change from a place that was mostly white and English-speaking to a place that encompasses almost every ethnic, linguistic and religious group on earth. The immigrants' impact is clearest in Toronto, which has been transformed. Toronto in the 1940s and 1950s was a city that insisted on not only the Puritan work ethic but an intensely private way of life; people entertained in their homes and usually lived most of their lives within one or two districts. In the 1980s, by contrast, the city is a kind of distant cultural outpost of continental Europe, an open and welcoming city, rich in cafes and restaurants and art galleries. It has a waterfront pleasure palace that does for Toronto what Tivoli does for Copenhagen and a large-scale indoor mall that shows the influence of Milan's galleria — both of them designed by a German immigrant architect. It has a city culture that tries to be simultaneously cosmopolitan and uniquely, independently Canadian. That's never an easy balance to strike, at a time when genuine independence of any kind for Canada is still an open question.

"Snow Ploughs in a Drift, On the Grand Trunk Railway" appeared in the
Canadian Illustrated News, 4 February 1871.

"Government House, from the Skating Pond," showing Rideau Hall, the residence of
Canada's governors-general, appeared in Picturesque Canada, Vol. I, 1882.

The most pessimistic view of modern Canadian history is that
Canada had only eight years of genuine independence—and they
were, as luck would have it, Depression years. This view holds
that with the Statute of Westminster (1931) Canada finally broke
free of England but that with the Ogdensburg Agreement (1940) it
finally acknowledged its utter dependence on the United States.
The Statute of Westminster, when passed by the British
parliament, legally recognized the self-governing dominions,
including Canada, as autonomous units. The Ogdensburg
Agreement, signed by President Franklin Roosevelt for the
United States and Prime Minister W.L.M. King for Canada,
established the Canada-United States Permanent Joint Board of
Defence. It set up a military alliance in which, inevitably, there
could be only one senior member and one junior member. And
Ogdensburg led naturally to the North American Air Defence
Agreement (NORAD), of 1957, in which Canada agreed to share
responsibility for air reconnaissance and defense systems for
North America.

Meanwhile, the ties with Britain were growing more and more
tenuous. The Liberal governments after the Second World

"Ottawa, Parliament Buildings from Major's Hill" appeared in
Picturesque Canada, Vol. I, 1882.

War—under W.L.M. King and his successor, Louis St. Laurent—
encouraged American penetration of the Canadian economy.
Canadians, particularly in Ontario, still spoke lovingly of the
British Commonwealth (the new, democratized name for the now
dead Empire), but they did so with an increasing sense of
nostalgia. The late Donald Creighton, the most eloquent of
nationalist historians, has written: "It became increasingly
obvious that neither the United Kingdom nor Canada regarded
the Commonwealth as the mainstay of its protection or
prosperity. Under Churchill and his successors, England sought
security in a special relationship with the United States and
began seriously to consider the economic advantages of
membership in the European Common Market. Canada was left
alone in North America, in the immediate presence of the greatest
military and industrial power on earth, a power which had
successfully grasped the leadership of the Western world." In

1971, Creighton declared: "The American Empire is taking over the birthright of Canadians; and its imperial religion has taken over their minds."

Those seeking support for that view could easily find it in the English-Canadian culture whose centre was southern Ontario. When television arrived in Ontario in 1952 it followed the American, not the British, model. Soon American programs were flowing over the border, backed by resources that in most cases quickly made them more popular than Canadian programs (British programs seldom appeared at all). Hollywood filled all but a few cinema screens. Canadian artists largely forgot England and looked to the United States for inspiration— novelists to figures like Norman Mailer and Saul Bellow, painters to American artists like Jackson Pollock and Willem de Kooning. American professors moved in to staff the new universities created in the 1960s by the demand for mass university education. Two successful performing arts organizations—the Shakespearean festival at Stratford, Ontario and the National Ballet, located in Toronto—remained under largely British leadership and worked according to British principles, but they were exceptions. For the most part, Toronto and the other cities of southern Ontario became cultural outposts of the United States. By the 1970s, when cable television was introduced, it was possible to see more American TV in southern Ontario than in many American cities. Even spectator sports—a component of Canadian identity since the popularization of hockey in the 1920s—were quickly being absorbed into the American system. The 1970s brought American major league baseball teams to Montreal and Toronto, and television carried most of the other mass sports of the United States to Canadian viewers.

There were moments, particularly in the early 1960s, when Canada seemed almost resigned to eventual absorption by the United States. This was particularly true during John Kennedy's presidency, when Canadians identified more with the glamorous political leadership in Washington than with their own politics in Ottawa. But in the late 1960s two factors produced a substantial change in the national mood—a change whose final impact will not be understood for a good many years.

The first factor was the development of a fresh view of Canadian politics by a group of intellectuals, artists, and politicians in southern Ontario, among them the politician Walter Gordon (who was federal finance minister in the early 1960s), the economist Melville Watkins, the poet and publisher Dennis Lee, and the philosopher George Grant. Though very different in many ways, they shared a suspicion of American influence and a desire for Canadian independence; they also assumed that Canadian independence must be achieved without substantial help from the British Commonwealth. In the euphoria created by the centennial of Confederation in 1967, their views spread rapidly.

The second factor, equally important, was the Vietnam War. In the Korean War, in the early 1950s, Canadians had fought alongside Americans as part of the United Nations force. This time, however, Canadians saw American policy in Asia as essentially wrong-headed. American anti-war sentiment found a quick response in Canada, and when thousands of American draft dodgers moved to Canada to avoid service in Vietnam, they were eagerly welcomed. By 1970 it became commonplace to refer to "the American empire", and Creighton—whose anti-Americanism had once isolated him from most of his contemporaries—was regarded as a prophet of Canadian independence.

Now Canadian culture became a battleground for the intellectuals. Ambitious plans were laid for a Canadian film industry, Canadian book publishing was generously supported by the federal (and in Ontario's case the provincial) government. Canadian theatre, also state-supported, produced a generation of playwrights who found a receptive audience. High schools staged "Canada Days" at which Canadian authors were celebrated, and "Canadian Studies" became an essential element in the curricula of universities, colleges and some high schools. For the first time, Canadian artists found themselves celebrated in their own country. The Toronto poet and novelist Margaret Atwood wrote a best-selling critical book, *Survival*, about the history of Canadian literature; she herself became a heroine of the nationalist movement, with a home market for her books that would be envied by most of the serious writers of the world. Pierre Berton, who had been a nationalist journalist in Toronto since the 1940s, produced a series of popular histories that pictured the Canadian past in dramatic and evocative terms; he became as a result the country's best-selling author.

For some of those involved in it, the nationalist celebration of Canadian culture was haunted by the spectre of another, earlier phase in history. In the 1920s Toronto was the centre of a nationalist movement that included publishing, theatre, music and above all painting. In those days, too, it was said that Canadian culture had come into its own, and that the Group of Seven landscape painters were the beginning of an indigenous form of cultural expression. The Group of Seven did prove permanently important to the life of the country (their paintings dominate a large museum, the McMichael Collection, north of Toronto) but most of the writers and musicians of that period were quickly forgotten and even the Group of Seven failed to influence the painters who followed them. When the Depression of the 1930s arrived, Canadian culture lost whatever place it had won in the country's imagination. The artists of the 1980s, while much better established than their predecessors of sixty years before, remain on shaky ground.

"Thunder Cape," a stormscape on Lake Superior, appeared in
Picturesque Canada, Vol. I, 1882.

Some large part of the Ontario population remained unimpressed by this long process; it saw the United States mainly as a spectacle rather than a threat, a society to be observed, admired, sometimes disliked. Marshall McLuhan, the most influential thinker produced by Ontario, once remarked: "Sharing the American way, without commitment to American goals or responsibilities, makes the Canadian intellectually detached and observant as an interpreter of the American destiny." Canadians were like connoisseurs of American reality, with front-row seats for the play of the century. But in recent decades, among influential groups in Ontario—and to a lesser extent elsewhere— this detachment turned into a fear of engulfment. As part of a nation-state that was created in reaction to the United States, the people of Ontario lived through the late twentieth century in the knowledge that the United States was, and perhaps always would be, the most important political, social, and cultural fact in their lives.

THE PRAIRIES

MANITOBA

SASKATCHEWAN

The Prairies

Manitoba
Area: 650,087
Population: 1,026,245
Capital: Winnipeg

Saskatchewan
Area: 651, 900 sq. km.
Population: 968, 310
Capital: Regina

Facing page. Tumbleweed, symbol of the open range in countless songs, stories and movies, comes about because the prairies, despite their fertility, have an essentially dry climate. When the stalks of various herbs and shrubs, especially sagebrush, as in this photograph, and the amaranths, become dessicated and break off from their root systems, they are tumbled into balls by the wind.

Above. St. Peter's Church stands on the bank of the Red River at Selkirk, Manitoba. The town is named for the Earl of Selkirk, who in the early 19th century bought a land tract almost the size of Great Britain from the Hudson's Bay Company. He established the Red River Settlement with crofters from the Scottish Highlands, and ushered in sixty years of rebellious struggle between white settlers and semi-nomadic Métis.

Above. The *Nonsuch*, a 36-foot ketch, was the first vessel to trade in Hudson Bay. She carried this carved figure on her forepeak. *Top. Golden Boy*, by the French sculptor Charles Gardet, decorates the dome of the neoclassic Manitoba Legislature *(facing page)*. The modern province grew out of Selkirk's Red River Settlement after the Canadian Pacific Railway opened a link to the East in 1885, bringing thousands of new settlers.

Previous page. Ponies graze on the shortgrass prairie within sight of the Cypress Hills, a gravel-conglomerate formation a hundred kilometres long that rises a thousand metres above the surrounding plain. When a party of ten American wolf hunters killed a dozen or more Canadian Indians here in 1873, the Canadian government formed the North West Mounted Police to bring the rule of law to the West. This force evolved into the RCMP — the famous red-coated Mounties who allegedly always get their man.

Above. Fire, flashing through dry grass and stubble, is a constant threat on the prairie. Lightning causes many fires, but some are man-made. Indian hunters once lit grass fires to drive buffalo. Today farmers use controlled fires, like the one pictured here, to remove stubble and return potash to soil.

Facing page. St. Michael's Ukrainian Orthodox Church, at Gardenton, Manitoba, was consecrated in 1899, the first such church in Canada. In many parts of the prairie, Ukrainians outnumbered all other pioneer groups. Clifford Sifton, the immigration minister of the period, called them "stalwart peasants in sheepskin coats." His agents were paid five dollars for each immigrating farmer, two dollars for each family member.

Before the pioneers broke the sod, the prairie grasslands were covered by at least 63 varieties, including four wild members of the wheat grass family. Hybrid wheat now occupies several million acres of prairie cropland. Coarse grains — oats, barley, and rye — and rape, a broadleafed flowering plant that yields oil from the seed, are the other principal cash crops.

Above. Constables of the Royal Canadian Mounted Police parade before their headquarters in Regina, Saskatchewan. Their celebrated red coats are today worn only on ceremonial occasions. Their first assignment, in the 1870s, was to run the lawless hunters and traders out of the whisky forts: Slideout, Robbers' Roost, Whisky Gap and the notorious Fort Whoop-Up.

Facing page. Church of Saint-Antoine-de-Padoue at Batoche, Saskatchewan, was occupied in March, 1885, by Louis Riel and his revolutionary council. From here they proclaimed a provisional government, thus launching the second Northwest Rebellion. Their first act was an ultimatum to the Mounted Police: leave the territory or face "a war of extermination." Three months later Riel and three hundred Métis followers, beseiged by 850 militiamen, surrendered; the rectory of the church at right is still scarred by bullet holes.

Left. The most populous prairie mammal is properly identified as Richardson's ground squirrel, but called by almost everybody the prairie gopher. Since gophers eat grain crops at every stage of development, their predators include farmers as well as hawks, badgers, weasels, coyotes, and rattlesnakes.

Previous page. The immensity of the empty plain is dramatized by the foreboding sky above this settler's house near Norwood, Saskatchewan. Such farmsteads are quickly disappearing as so-called "industrial" farming organizations assemble larger tracts of land.

Above. The first habitation built by many pioneers was a sod house, much like this restoration. In the Ukrainian variety, called a *boorday*, the farmer dug a metre-deep pit, lined it with upright logs and roofed it with aspen branches covered by sod. Among English-speaking settlers the sod roofing squares were known as "prairie shingles".

Facing page. Regina (named for Queen Victoria) became the capital of Saskatchewan when the new province joined the Canadian confederation in 1905. The domed legislature, seen breaking the skyline in this photograph, is surrounded by formal gardens and fountains, including one from London's Trafalgar Square. Riel, leader of the Northwest Rebellions, was tried in Regina and hanged there for treason on Nov. 16, 1885.

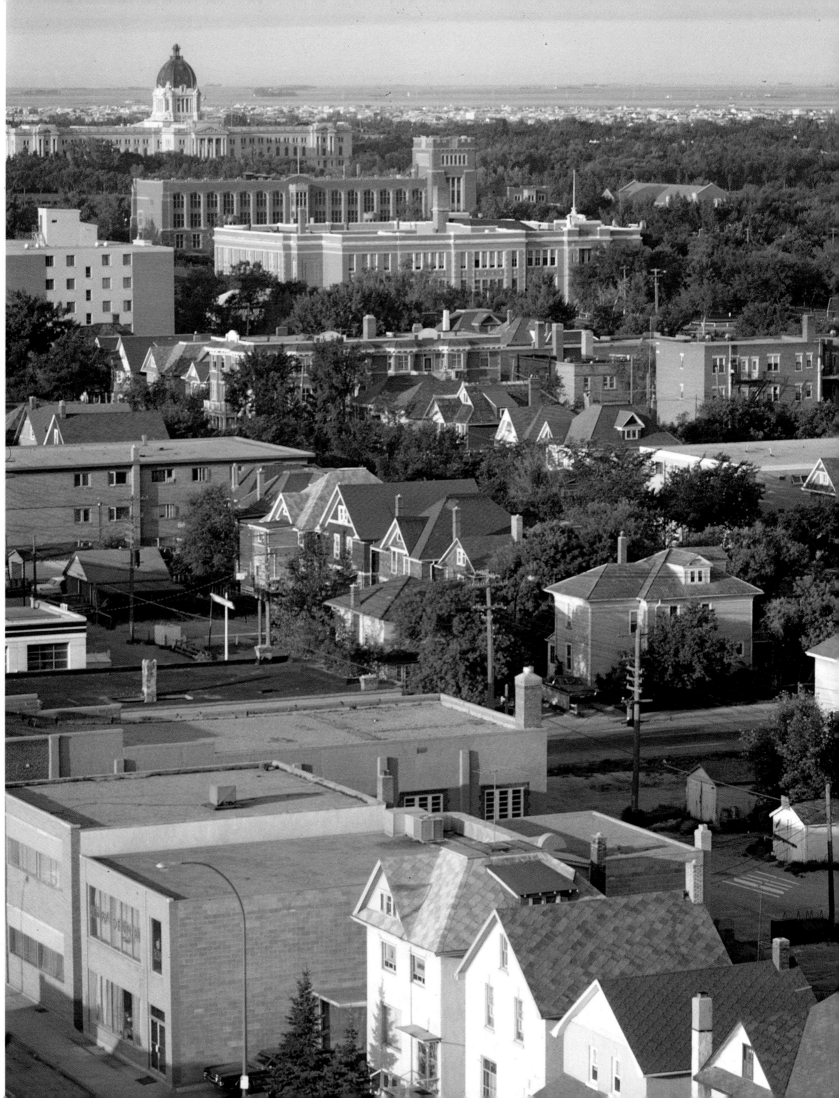

THE PRAIRIES

"Red River Cart and Ox," a pencil drawing executed by Paul Kane in 1846,
is in the Royal Ontario Museum, Toronto.

we ran west
wanting a place of absolute
unformed beginning...
— Margaret Atwood

In 1880 J.G. Donkin, a corporal with the North West Mounted
Police (later called the Royal Canadian Mounted Police), set down
an account of his experiences in a book for English readers,
Trooper and Redskin. He described the Canadian prairies as they
unfolded before the astonished eyes of the easterners and Europeans who confronted them.

"There is the hush of an eternal silence hanging over these far
stretching plains. In early summer, for a brief space, the prairie is
green, with shooting threads of gold, scarlet and blue... But, by
and by, the sun gains power, and scorches, and withers, with a

Facing page. By 1904, more than a million
migrants had changed the face of the prairie,
often bringing the cultural styles of Europe
with them. This Greek Orthodox Church was
built in that year at Shishovchi, Saskatchewan.

157

furnace heat; and through the shimmering haze the grass lies gray and dead. And, under the merciless glare, a great silence broods over all . . . No tree or bush relieves the aching eye: there is nothing but the dim fading ring of the horizon all around . . . You may blindfold a man in places, and take him to another spot a hundred miles away; removing his bandage I would wager he would think he had travelled around to his starting point."

This was the unpromising landscape in which tens of thousands of immigrants found themselves late in the nineteenth and early in the twentieth centuries. This unwelcoming, featureless plain was the territory they had to make habitable, and perhaps some day profitable, for themselves and their children. This was the country that eventually turned into the provinces of Manitoba and Saskatchewan—provinces that today, a century later, are prosperous and settled, with all the civilized amenities of modern life.

The struggle to develop the West is one of the epic sagas of the Canadian experience and it remains today a part of the folk memory of the people. In Ontario, the days of the pioneers are long in the past, consigned to the history books; but in a western city like Winnipeg, Manitoba or Regina, Saskatchewan, there are many thousands of people who have heard from their own grandparents about the years of bitter deprivation and desperately hard work. The accomplishment of the pioneers still colors the imagination and the political life of the West, still fuels its pride and its sense of grievance against the East. Unlike the Maritimes and Central Canada, the West remains psychologically a frontier society.

In a sense, the West carries through modern times a feeling of historic victimization that parallels the sentiments of French-Canadians. Westerners tend to believe that, through Canadian history, they have been manipulated and used by distant powers over which they have little or no control. The very fact of Confederation seems in many ways part of that victimization. In 1946 the most distinguished Manitoba historian, W.L. Morton, wrote: "Confederation was brought about to increase the wealth of Central Canada, and until that original purpose is altered, and the concentration of wealth and population by national policy in Central Canada ceases, Confederation must remain an instrument of injustice." Since then the West has grown far richer in many ways—the booming national prosperity of the 1950s and 1960s spread to most of the towns and cities on the prairies. But the sense of grievance remains alive, and most of articulate western opinion today would still agree in substance with Morton's 1946 opinion.

Partly because of this belief, the West has been the setting for some of the most important innovation in Canada. The Winnipeg General Strike of 1919, which many Canadians briefly saw as the introduction of Soviet-style communism into Canada, became in the end a milestone on the road toward the establishment of trade unionism across the country. In the 1920s the West sent to the federal parliament representatives of the Progressive Party, who pressed for social reform and pushed the dominant Liberal Party toward progressive measures. In the early 1930s the Progressives turned into the Co-operative Commonwealth Federation, which formed the government of Saskatchewan—the first democratic socialist government in North American history—in 1944. In the 1960s the CCF re-organized itself, now with substantial backing from organized labor, as the New Democratic Party; under that name it has since formed governments in Saskatchewan, Manitoba and British Columbia and played a vital role as the third party in the federal parliament. Western populism has taken other forms than socialism. In the 1930s in Alberta the Social Credit Party—loosely based on the eccentric monetary ideas of the British theorist Clifford Douglas—came to power in Alberta and maintained its hold on the province for more than three decades. Social Credit also became for a time a serious force in national politics and took power in British Columbia. A third strain of western populism appeared in the person of John Diefenbaker, of Saskatchewan, who temporarily converted the federal Progressive Conservative Party to his populist views and served as prime minister of Canada from 1957 to 1963.

These political forces, which have helped set the public tone of life in Canada for more than half a century, have in common a belief that the conditions of life for westerners are unfairly dictated by distant, elite powers. At various times those powers may be identified as the eastern banks, the railways, the federal government, the international food-processing corporations, or the rich traders on the grain exchanges. Whatever their precise nature, they are seen as coldly unresponsive to the needs of the western people, and the most important impulses of western politi-

"Louis Riel," a contemporary portrait of the rebel leader.

"Red River Expedition at Shebaunaning," sketched with the
military force despatched to put down the first Northwest Rebellion, appeared in the
Canadian Illustrated News, 16 July 1870.

cal life are directed toward setting right the injustices that these
various national systems impose.

This theme stretches back far beyond Confederation, the railroad, and national tariff policies—right back, in fact, to the first
European settlements in the West. In the beginning the West was
ruled not by a government at all but by the seventeenth century
equivalent of a multi-national corporation—"The Governor and
Company of Adventurers of England trading into Hudson's Bay,"
as its first charter called it. Later it became known as the Hudson's Bay Company, and its descendant company still exists
today as a diversified corporation with interests in department
stores (called "The Bay") and many other fields. It began life in
1670 with a British royal charter giving it power over a vaguely
defined territory that covered all the lands draining into Hudson
Bay; eventually this was stretched as far west as Vancouver
Island, off the Pacific coast of Canada.

The Company had no interest in developing agriculture in the
vast lands it governed. From the beginning its concern was furs

for sale in Europe, and to gather them it set up trading posts across the West—little communities which determined the location of the Indian tribes trading with the Company and later of the major cities of western Canada. For two centuries the Company held an official monopoly in its territory and in its late years persistently fought off the incursions of American traders from the south. But by the middle of the nineteenth century, as Canadians began to dream of a nation stretching to the Pacific, the Company's peculiar role came to be seen as increasingly anachronistic. In 1869 the Company sold most of its property to Canada for 300,000 British pounds. The way was cleared for Confederation and the development of the West under democratic government.

At that moment, most of the settlers in the West were British or French, but soon the pattern of immigration began to change. In the 1870s the government began attracting settlers from eastern Europe—between 1874 and 1878, for example, it brought some 6,000 Mennonites from the Czarist Ukraine by promising freedom, exemption from military service, and a block of land in the Red River Valley in what is now Manitoba. These first attempts to bring in non-French and non-British settlers were the beginnings of what Canadians now call "multi-culturalism." Ukrainians, Russians, Germans, Icelanders, and Belgians followed. In some cases they consciously settled in one place—in the 1870s and 1880s, for example, Icelandic immigrants gathered near Gimli, Manitoba, which today remains Icelandic in character. In many other cases they formed into ethnic associations based on shared language and religious backgrounds. Their attachment to their roots gave the West the special ethnic character it has maintained throughout this century.

In the 1880s the building of the Canadian Pacific Railway and the development of early-maturing wheat strains (suited to the brief growing season) encouraged the spread of agriculture over the prairies. The transformation was slow, however, until 1896. That was the year Sir Clifford Sifton of Winnipeg went to Ottawa as minister of the interior in Sir Wilfred Laurier's government. He had criticized the immigration policies of the federal government as slow-witted and short-sighted: now he took the responsibility for those policies. He stayed in the government until 1905 and presided over the crucial years in the opening of the West, helping to make it (as one of his government slogans called it) "The World's Bread Basket." In all of Canadian history, no other single politicians has had such a formative influence on the social geography of a Canadian region.

Sifton's closest friends never suggested that he was idealistically interested in social reform; nor did they claim for him any compassionate feelings for the poor of Europe. A lawyer and a financier, he was interested in the prosperity of himself and others like him. He saw the settlement of the West as the key to Canadian economic health.

In Sifton's view, the best immigrants would be Americans, who might bring in capital as well as North American agricultural skills. He attracted some of them, but they were not available in sufficient numbers. He was less inclined than his predecessors toward British immigrants, partly because Britain was so heavily urbanized and partly because the British were showing too much interest in trade unionism. Sifton wanted tough and determined farming people, and he turned his attention to the peasant heartland of Europe. He sent agents to the Ukraine, Poland, Hungary and Rumania in search of potential immigrants. He made immigration a national crusade, and spoke of immigrants bluntly, in terms of their use to Canada and their "quality", rather as if they were livestock. As he wrote—"I think a stalwart peasant in a sheep-skin coat, born on the soil, whose forefathers have been farmers for ten generations, with a stout wife and a half-dozen children, is good quality."

Attracted by advertising and the promise of free land, the settlers poured in. In 1904 a local historian in Rosthern, Saskatchewan, noted that its people included Galicians, Hungarians (speaking Slovak and Magyar), Hungarian Orthodox and Reform Jews, German Catholics, French Canadians, and Doukhobors from Russia. There were many such communities in the new west.

But not everyone in Canada was pleased. The immigrant peasants were sometimes given the nickname "Sifton's sheepskins," and those who believed firmly in the British connection were appalled by the sudden appearance on the prairies of tens of thousands of immigrants to whom the English language was foreign. In some years, during Sifton's time, half of the immigrants passing through Winnipeg were Slavs. Conservative politicians and newspapers attacked Sifton, but his views prevailed. When he left office in 1905 he was acknowledged as the architect of western development.

The settlers themselves, most of them only dimly aware of the political and economic planning that brought them to Canada, were enduring isolation and hardship. They were given land, or sold it cheaply, but making that land livable seemed at times almost impossible. The "homesteads" on which they were deposited were usually virgin land. One man, who arrived at his homestead in 1904, later wrote: "I'll never forget the desolate feeling that came over me, when, with the contents of the wagon out on the ground, we sat on a box and looked around, not a sign of any other human habitation or a road leading to one to be seen, nothing but bluff and water and grass. Then I realized that we were at the end of our journey, that this was to be our home, that if we wanted a house to cover us, a stable for our horses, a well for drinking water, it would have to be the work of our own hands."

Many of the settlers spent their first winters in sod huts, made by using chunks of sod dug out of the earth as building blocks. Insects and dirt fell from the ceiling and the walls, the cold blew in and an inch or more of frost might gather on the inside of the windows. Outside the huts there was work so hard that it could sap a man's or woman's youth; often the settlers grew old before their time. But the worst hardship was isolation. Many of the immigrant farmers came from densely settled parts of Europe and brought with them a need for community; now they found themselves scattered across the sparsely settled prairies. They endured because they had no choice and because they believed they were creating a fresh society that would eventually give their sacrifice meaning. And, in this new environment, they did make a society with new standards. An immigrant came to be judged— and judged others—not by possessions or family or accent but by the ability to survive.

Eventually the farms were developed and survival was no longer the main issue of life. The need for community asserted itself and farmers drew together in co-operatives to market their grain. Isolation was replaced by interdependence. The 1930s brought the last era of desperation, when disastrously low commodity prices on the world markets combined with drought to push many farmers into bankruptcy. The Second World War, and the post-war boom, transformed the West again.

Today a visitor to western Canada will encounter brisk, clean cities filled with prosperous-looking citizens who seem not noticeably different from their contemporaries in the East. The shopping malls around Winnipeg look much like the shopping malls in southern Ontario, and the curriculum at the University of Saskatchewan differs only a little from the curriculum at the University of Western Ontario. The Canadian West has a sophisticated, urban culture. There are good theatre companies in most of the cities; there are excellent writers and painters scattered all over the West. But if you drive a few miles from any city, onto the prairie, the same "hush of an eternal silence" that Corporal Donkin saw in the 1880s remains. And it lingers, too, in the culture of the West. The painters play endless creative variations on prairie light, the writers probe deeper and deeper into the experience of pioneer life, and the most successful play written in western Canada in the last decade was a musical comedy about the wheat co-ops in which prairie isolation was a constant theme. The West, in its politics and culture, even in everyday conversation, is not far from the pioneer experience that began to take shape a century ago.

ALBERTA

Alberta
Area: 661, 185 sq. km.
Population: 2,237, 725
Capital: Edmonton

FORTIS · ET · LIBER

Facing page. Alberta's Waterton Lakes National Park lies on the border between Canada and the United States, adjoining Montana's Glacier National Park. In 1932 the two countries linked them, to form the world's first International Peace Park. The Waterton Lakes park lies on the frontier between the Rocky Mountains and the Prairies, as does much of Alberta.

Previous page. The Bow River rises in the Rockies near the famous resort at Banff and flows through the foothills to Alberta's largest city, Calgary, on the edge of the Prairie. The river valley was scoured by the last receding glacier, about ten thousand years ago, which also left behind many eskers and moraines, the characteristic landforms of a post-glacial region. Fishermen on the Bow take several kinds of trout: cut-throat, brown, brook, rainbow.

Left. Lake Louise, still as pretty as the millions of postcards this scene has inspired, lies north of Banff in the same national park. From lake level Canada's longest aerial tramway, 3.2 km., rises 400 metres to a lookout point on Whitehorn Mountain.

Facing page. After drilling 133 dry holes, Canada's largest oil company, Imperial, struck oil here in 1947. The well, where this donkey-head rocker pump has been left in place ever since, was named Leduc No. 1. By the 1980s Alberta had more than twenty thousand oil and gas wells.

Stoney Indians play the bone game, (*above*), an ancient form of gambling akin to dice. The name of the tribe comes from the custom of cooking on heated stones. Stoneys are part of the great Cree-speaking grouping of Plains Indians; their teepees, head-dresses and decorative arts are in the tradition of this group, which includes the Blackfoot tribes and Hollywood's favourite Indians, the Sioux. For ten days every July the Stoneys, too, go into show business as they add their vivid presence to the Calgary Stampede, the largest rodeo in the West.

Premier event at the Calgary Stampede is the heart-stopping chuck wagon race — four wagons, twenty outriders, thirty-two horses all careening toward the same finishing line. The Stampede is a show known round the world, with nightly street dances, fireworks, grandstand variety shows, midways and casinos, thoroughbred horse racing and livestock competitions in addition to the rodeo.

Cowboys (and girls) compete in bronco riding, with and without saddles, bull riding, wild-cow milking, buffalo riding, calf-throwing and a wild-horse race — with, in all, a quarter of a million dollars in prizes.

Fort Calgary, forerunner of the modern city,
was built in 1875 as a Mounted Police post.
During most of its first century the economy
was based on cattle and the most active market
was the daily auction at the downtown
stockyards. But as the Albertan oil fields
developed, so did Calgary's influence as the
administrative and financial centre of the
petroleum industry. By the beginning of the
1980s Calgary was Canada's most dynamic
city, its wealth, population and skyline all
rising dramatically. From a city park, however,
a grazing mountain sheep can still see on the
horizon its ancestral home a hundred kilometres away in the Rockies.

Edmonton, the capital of Alberta, is Calgary's near-twin in size (both have about half a million people) but polar opposite in orientation. Where Calgarians look south to the Texan style of mixing oil and money, Edmontonians tend to look north to the austere but mineral-rich frontier. Physically the city bestrides the great North Saskatchewan River, where Fort Edmonton was built as a Hudson's Bay Company fur trading post in the 1790s. Almost on the same site now stands the Legislative Building.

Left, Number 99, Wayne Gretzky, one of the world's greatest hockey players, is a forward for the Edmonton Oilers.

Above. Across the border between Alberta and the Northwest Territories sprawls the largest park in the world, Wood Buffalo National Park. Here roams the last sizable herd — about 12,000 individuals — of bison or North American buffalo.

Left. Albertan croplands, often better watered than the dry-belt prairie to the east, include many of Canada's highest yielding and most consistently productive farms. In the mixed-farming regions near Edmonton some families claim the crops have never failed.

Overleaf. The Red Deer Badlands, an eerie eroded sandstone valley lying between the towns of Drumheller and Brooks, has some of the most varied fossil remains in the world.

ALBERTA

"Moose Deer of North America" appeared in Travels Through the Canadas, 1807.

The energy crisis of the 1970s became an obsession to most of the industrialized countries of the world, but in Canada it had a special meaning. The issues surrounding oil and gas resources threw a harsh light on national differences and threatened Confederation in a way that no other problem except language has done in recent years. They brought the phrase "western alienation" into the Canadian language, aroused long-dormant fears of western separatism, and changed fundamentally the status of the province of Alberta.

Facing page. The Badlands (*see also pages 178/9*) appear from a distance to be entirely barren, but they do support many forms of desert life, including lizards and insects, sagebrush, saskatoon and chokecherry, and several kinds of cactus. The plains prickly pear bears a delicate yellow flower like a small rose, the purple cactus has a reddish-mauve blossom with a pineapple-shaped heart.

The province that begins as prairie and parkland at the Saskatchewan border and then reaches into the Rocky Mountains, Alberta has always had a unique character. From the early years of the century—Alberta became a province in 1905—it has been characterized by a spirit of individualism and free enterprise. Unlike the three other western provinces, it has never elected a socialist government or shown any signs of doing so. Its vast cat-

"Near Fort Calgary, Looking Toward the Rocky Mountains" appeared in Picturesque Canada, Vol. I, 1882. Artist was the Marquis of Lorne, then Governor General of Canada.

tle ranches and oil fields remind many Americans of their own southwest, and on the streets of Calgary today you can often hear the drawl of recent immigrants from Texas. An American businessman may feel something of a stranger in Ottawa or Regina, but he feels at home almost anywhere in Alberta..

Even more than the other western provinces, Alberta has been fueled by a mood of optimism. Its unofficial motto for many years was "Tomorrow Country," and its leading politicians have always spoken of a golden and gleaming future. The immigrants it attracted seventy or eighty years ago, both from the United States and Europe, developed a passionate belief in good times to come and produced many a local boom. In 1911 a journalist wrote of the founding of Mirror, Alberta, in a way that suggested the hectic atmosphere of the period. "When the town site of Mirror was first placed on the market," he wrote, ". . . there were 577 lots sold at auction in 660 minutes. The aggregate purchase prices of these lots was $250,000. That was the beginning. Many more lots have been sold since. Before Mirror was a month old it had two banks, five stores, three lumber yards, one hotel, three restaurants, two pool rooms, a sash and door factory and a newspaper. When it reaches the mature age of one year it will be a wonder."

Mirror, like many another hopeful little town, never did develop into a metropolis, but the same kind of booming spirit has occurred in Alberta again and again. In the great Depression of the 1930s, when the bottom dropped out of the market for Alberta wheat and beef cattle and other commodities, the province's voters turned in rage and bewilderment to an optimistic and messianic politician who remains unique in Canadian history: William (Bible Bill) Aberhart (1878–1943) was both an evangelical Christian and the energetic prophet of a new form of economics. A schoolteacher and the founder of the Calgary Prophetic Bible Institute, he was attracted to the radical monetary ideas articulated under the name "Social Credit" by a British engineer, C.H. Douglas, the same ideas that became one of the principal interests of the mad American poet Ezra Pound. Aberhart, like Douglas, blamed hard times on the world's bankers. "Food is rotting in warehouses, being burned and dumped into the sea," he declared in 1932. "It is the money system destroying food to maintain prices." Aberhart and the Social Credit Party promised to redistribute purchasing power and create a money system that would bring prosperity to Alberta and eventually spread to dozens of other countries. In 1935 he and the Social Credit Party campaigned with the slogan "The Eyes of the World Are On Alberta," and triumphantly took office. His attempts at monetary reform were soon frustrated—banking was a federal rather than a provincial responsibility, and the bankers were therefore beyond Aberhart's grasp. But he and his successors, most of them right-wing Christians, stayed in office for thirty-six years. Next door in Saskatchewan, the Co-operative Commonwealth Federation was creating a moderate socialist revolution which would eventually influence the whole country, but Albertans favoured a more conservative government, then as now.

By the time Social Credit was voted out, in 1971, Alberta was on the way to a brief period of prosperity unequalled by any large area in Canadian history. In terms of jobs, private fortunes, construction and general giddy optimism, nothing like it had ever happened before; perhaps nothing like it will ever happen again. At the height of the boom, in the late 1970s, "Alberta" and "rich" were almost synonyms to Canadians.

In its early stages the development of modern Alberta was part of the post-war boom that touched most areas of Canada, but at its climax it was centered on oil and natural gas—real oil, and real natural gas coming out of the ground, and potential oil and natural gas that might, by a stretch of the imagination, come out of the ground in the near future if the price turned out to be right.

Oil in some quantity was discovered in the Turner Valley near Calgary in 1914, but Alberta did not become a major oil producer until 1947, one of the two key years in the province's modern development (the other being 1973, the start of the OPEC price rises). On February 13, 1947, a few miles north-east of the town of Leduc (which is not far south of Edmonton), an Imperial Oil crew, after ten weeks of drilling, struck large quantities of high-quality crude oil. Imperial Leduc No. 1, as the well was called, became an event in Canadian history and folklore, told and re-told over the years (there were many stories, for instance, about the fact that the crew almost gave up in despair just before hitting Leduc No. 1). The oil that came out at Leduc was important in itself (that well didn't go dry until 1974) but even more important for what it indicated about the possibilities of oil nearby. In the next quarter of a century Alberta became an important centre of the petroleum business. In Calgary (which was founded in the nineteenth century as a Northwest Mounted Police fort) corporations sprang up, and large branch offices of the multi-national oil firms expanded. By 1979, 512 of the 612 Canadian-based exploration and production companies in the oil business had their head offices in Calgary. Alberta produced a generation of scientists and entrepreneurs who spread the province's influence far beyond the boundaries of Canada—Alberta firms helped develop North Sea oil, for example, and played a role in the Middle East. Calgary became a magnet drawing businessmen, geologists and ordinary workers from all over the continent. Edmonton, which had started life as a Hudson's Bay Company trading post and is the capital of the province, served as a supply centre for the new oil developments in the north; it experienced a similar boom.

These tendencies, already under way in the 1950s and the 1960s, picked up speed in the 1970s, after the first oil shock hit the world economy and all energy became much more expensive. Alberta not only had most of the oil available in Canada, it had even more that was not yet obtainable but might soon be. For two centuries people had known of the dark, oil-saturated sands along the Athabasca River near Fort McMurray in northeastern Alberta. Now, with the price of oil rising, and apparently destined to rise forever, the Athabasca tar sands became the focus of attention. It was said that they contained the world's largest deposit of oil, and at the new prices, separating the oil from the sand would for the first time be worthwhile. A gigantic project was undertaken jointly by the governments of Canada, Alberta and Ontario and the multi-national oil companies.

These and parallel developments in natural gas and coal sent a wave of happy anticipation through the Canadian economy. Everyone would benefit—Maritimers were moving to Fort McMurray for jobs, Toronto banks and stock brokerages were setting up gleaming new offices in Calgary and Edmonton, the steel mills in Hamilton, Ontario were waiting to make the steel for the new pipelines that would be needed. Prosperity would radiate out from Alberta to British Columbia on the west and to much of Canada on the east. There was something for everyone in the Alberta

"Half Breeds Running Buffalo" is from an 1846 oil painting by Paul Kane,
which is now in the Royal Ontario Museum.

"Indian Trappers of the North-West" appeared in Picturesque Canada, Vol. I, 1882.

oil boom, or there soon would be. And Alberta had moved from the periphery to the centre of Canadian consciousness.

But if this development was economically exciting, it was politically painful. Once again a provincial government was pitted against Ottawa; once again a region of Canada believed itself cheated by the federal authorities; once again the historic push-pull of Confederation was acted out in meeting after meeting, angry statement after angry statement.

At the centre of the controversy was the price Alberta was to charge Canadians for oil. Put simply, Alberta wanted the price high and the rest of Canada wanted it low. The price was set in Ottawa, after negotiations with Edmonton, and it was kept well below the quickly rising world price. This, in Alberta's eyes, was manifestly unfair.

Partly because their winters are so cold, and partly because they routinely drive their large cars long distances, Canadians are the most voracious energy-users in the world. So it followed that through the 1970s and the early 1980s, energy was at the centre of the economic problems of Pierre Trudeau's federal government; and Alberta oil was seen as the key to solving those problems. Ottawa put an export tax on oil leaving the country (which infuriated Alberta), it created its own major oil company, Petrocan (which infuriated both Alberta and the private oil companies), and finally with its National Energy Policy of 1980 it set seriously about the task of "Canadianizing" the oil industry; that is, bringing some large part of it under Canadian rather than American ownership. All of this was done in the name of "energy self-sufficiency."

The Ottawa policies, and Alberta's response to them, posed a question that went to the heart of Confederation—who owned the oil? From Ottawa's standpoint, the oil was a Canadian resource, to be used to benefit all Canadians. From Alberta's, it was an Alberta resource, the treasure that the pioneers of Alberta had accidentally staked as their own.

For Albertans, oil came to represent both their pride and their future; one Canadian scholar, after a long analysis of the question, claimed that the energy issue was fully as important to Alberta as the French language was to Quebec. Albertans saw the oil bonanza as a historic, once-in-a-century chance to diversify their economy and provide for the welfare of their children and grandchildren. At last Alberta, if allowed to sell its oil at a fair price, would have a capital base on which it could build a secure future. But Ontario and Quebec wanted cheap energy to run factories and cars, and heat homes—and, in one way or another, Ontario and Quebec, as the most populous provinces, controlled the actions of the federal government.

186

This became the basis for "western alienation," the most pressing challenge to Confederation since the rise of Quebec separatism in the 1960s. Alberta even had a minor political party which included the possibility of separatism in its platform (separatism, for Alberta, would presumably mean joining the United States), and during a severe oil shortage a few Alberta cars carried bumper stickers saying, "Let the eastern bastards freeze in the dark." More important, Albertans had no sympathy with the Liberal Party which had governed Canada during most years in the last five decades. Alberta supported the Progressive Conservative Party, and year after year it watched its members of parliament go to Ottawa and sit impotently on the opposition benches. For one brief period, in 1979–1980, an Albertan, Joe Clark, led a Progressive Conservative minority government in Ottawa; but his government fell and the Trudeau Liberals returned. Except for Clark's nine months in office, Albertans have not felt properly represented in Ottawa for at least a generation.

Premier Peter Lougheed, whose Conservative government displaced Social Credit in 1971, made Ottawa his chief enemy in each election campaign and articulated, year after year, the grievances of the Albertans. He promised to build the provincial economy (he put some of the oil profits into the Alberta Heritage Fund, an investment base) while at the same time insisting that Ottawa was making his task impossible. Like most Albertans, he looked with apprehension at a distant point in the future when energy resources would run out and Alberta would return to the old boom-and-bust cycle that had traditionally plagued the western provinces of Canada.

But economic disaster turned out to be much closer than even the most pessimistic Albertan imagined. The world recession of the early 1980s turned the oil shortage into an oil glut, drove down the price of oil everywhere, and brought some of Alberta's most ambitious oil-extraction projects to a sudden halt. In Calgary it seemed to happen almost overnight. On one day there were plans for construction and expansion everywhere; all the companies were hiring workers. A day later—or so it appeared in dazed retrospect—the construction was stopped and the corporations were firing their employees. As one property developer put it, "In Calgary, there's panic in the streets." For the moment, at least, Alberta's brief period as the centre of economic activity in Canada was over.

THE ARCTIC

NORTHWEST TERRITORIES

YUKON TERRITORY

The Arctic
The Northwest Territories
Area: 3,379, 684 sq. km.
Population: 45,740
Capital: Yellowknife
Yukon Territory
Area: 482,515 sq. km.
Population: 23,150
Capital: Whitehorse

Facing page. While the line that separates the North and the true Arctic is not clearly drawn, most Canadians would agree that the Arctic begins somewhere on the Canadian Shield near the divide between the east, west and south flowing river systems and those that flow to Hudson Bay and the Arctic Ocean. This immense empty land mass is linked between scattered settlements only by bush planes, so called because the first bush pilots flew not far above tree level, navigating by following known landmarks much like Indians and traders of earlier times. This plane, a Norseman, uses pontoons for water landings in summer, and switches to skis for ice landings in winter.

Facing page. Dawson, at the junction of the Yukon and Klondike Rivers, has fewer than a thousand permanent residents. Between 1896 and the turn of the century, at the height of the great Klondike Gold Rush, there were 40,000 people here and the world referred to Dawson as "The City of Gold." Much of the boomtown past has been recreated: Canada's only legal casino, Diamond-Tooth Gertie's Gambling Hall; the Palace Grand Theatre where the *Gaslight Follies* are staged each summer; and a score of hotels, saloons and dance halls.

Sea-lions (*top*) are the largest members of the seal family. Although their fur-colour is not unlike the African lion's, they take their name from the sound they make, a deep, roaring bark. A large male sea-lion might weigh five hundred kilos, while a male walrus (*below*) might weigh twice as much. The walrus is a separate species, identified by large tusks prized by Eskimo artists as material for ivory carvings.

Overleaf. The magnificent Mackenzie River runs 4,200 km. to the Arctic Ocean. Like other great rivers, it has a branching delta with many mouths.

Above. The Arctic environment brings about some of the most striking survival adaptations in the entire animal kingdom. The snowy owl is almost invisible against snow, ice, or Arctic sky. The polar bear, equally at home on land, in the ocean, or on drifting ice, can withstand water temperatures that would destroy most land mammals. But hunting pressure has reduced its numbers; the great white bear has been placed on the world list of endangered species by the International Union for Conservation of Nature in Switzerland.

Facing page. Sled dogs, called "huskies" by Southerners, can belong to any one of four breeds — the Eskimo, Malamute, Samoyed or Siberian husky. On long journeys, dog teams can pull heavily laden sleds at a steady eight kilometres an hour. Racing, they reach speeds four times as great.

Overleaf. The last great ice sheet that 18,000 years ago covered nearly all Canada originated among the Arctic Islands. The most northerly of these, Ellesmere Island, lies just west of Greenland; its northern cape is the closest point of land to the geographic north pole. Looking at Ellesmere's permanent glaciers today is much like looking at Europe or mid-North America during the Ice Age.

Left. Tides rise and fall almost ten metres at Lake Harbour in the Northwest Territories. As the tide rises, the water adds another thickness of ice on the shoreline. Local people call this effect an "ice elevator."

Right. Busiest and perhaps best-known of the Eskimo print-making shops is at Cape Dorset. Contemporary Eskimo arts are based on traditional skills: carving in stone to make oil lamps and cooking pots, carving in bone or ivory to make tools and weapons. Since the 1950s, Eskimo artists have added to their range drawing and print-making, painting in oils and watercolours, and ceramics. Working with these new materials and techniques, they have developed what some critics believe to be a new form: "the art of the new Eskimo."

Left. The geology of the high Arctic suggests major oil discoveries to be made both on and off shore. But exploration is arduous, expensive — and so far inconclusive. Not enough oil has yet been found to justify the tens of billions of dollars that would be needed to construct a production and distribution system. Yet some wells are promising: this one, Imperial Oil's Issungniak well, was drilled into the sea bed from a small man-made island, and gives good quantities of both oil and gas.

Right. An Eskimo summer camp, on the shore of a stream that empties into the Arctic Ocean, is today an exotic blend of the stone age with the machine age. This group arrived here in boats powered by outboard motors. But the stone weirs that trap the fish before they are speared belong to the earliest Eskimo culture.

THE ARCTIC

"Arctic Navigation" was commissioned for The Polar World, 1874.

Facing page. Furs first drew outsiders to the north, and despite the modern advent of aircraft, snowmobiles and oil-exploration crews, the master image of the region remains a solitary Cree hunter walking his trapline on snowshoes, his dog drawing his pack sled.

For generations Canadians have told each other that their future lies in the North, and a leading historian wrote that "Canada is a northern country with a northern economy, a northern way of life and a northern destiny." The North is Canada's permanent frontier, and it sits heavily on top of the Canadian imagination—the place of mystery and magic and romance, the geographic location of the Canadian unconscious. Some of the most powerful works of art ever created in Canada are Lawren Harris's paintings of Arctic mountains, paintings which most Canadians first see in childhood and remember all their lives. There is no Canadian who fails to recognize in some way the importance of the Eskimos, those few thousand native northerners. Certainly one can't go to school in Canada, or watch much Canadian television, without learning of the traditionally nomadic Eskimo way of life based on trapping animals and catching fish. Everyone who grows up in Canada lives with an image of the lonely white snow-bound vastness of the North and hears often of the land where in winter there is no day and in summer there is no night. The identity of Canadians depends on their sense of the North.

"Spearing the Walrus" is from The Polar World, 1874.

And yet to most Canadians the real North is little more than an elaborate rumor. Only a tiny minority of Canadians have ever visited the North, and hardly anyone has actually settled there. About one quarter of one per cent of Canadians live in the Yukon and the Northwest Territories, the two administrative districts into which most of the country north of the 60th parallel is divided. Eskimos, Indians, Métis and whites, they add up to a few more than seventy thousand people, enough to fill a good-sized football stadium. The territory they occupy amounts to 3.8 million sq. km., about forty per cent of Canada. But nearly all the people can be found in about seventy-five communities, the largest of which—Whitehorse, the Yukon capital—has a population of seventeen thousand. From an aircraft, most of the North is uninhabited and seems uninhabitable.

Paradoxically, though, it teems with life. Caribou, polar bears, lemmings, Arctic foxes and large white hares roam the land and the sea ice. In the sea itself are whales, walruses and seals. About seventy-five species of birds fly to the Arctic to breed in the short summer. Some eight hundred different flowering plants and ferns can be found in the Arctic. Purple fireweed and bright orange lichen cover the hillsides. In the winter it is cold, though not as cold as Siberia: the lowest temperature ever recorded in the North was minus 62 Celsius at Snag, Yukon, in February 1947. In the world's imagination, snow always covers the North, but in fact the land more closely resembles a frozen desert. Some regions have as little precipitation as Cairo, and in some a whole winter may bring as little snow as falls in Montreal in the course of a single day.

In recent decades the North has become a political and economic battlefield, fought over by multi-national corporations, the federal government, the governing councils of the Yukon and the Northwest Territories, and the organizations representing native rights. The Eskimos (who nowadays are usually called Inuit, the term they prefer) have claimed the central and eastern area of the Northwest Territories above the treeline: they call this "Nunavut", which means "our land", and they want to exert political control over it. The Dene Indians, located in the Mackenzie River Valley, want political control over their territory, to be held in common with the people of mixed Indian-white ancestry known as Métis. In the Yukon, the Council for Yukon Indians is asking for outright ownership of lands for native communities, exclusive hunting, trapping and fishing rights, compensation for past use of Indian land, and a share in resource development. The white settlers, on the other hand, and the great corporations employing them, want the right to use the North's resources in their own way.

What no one disagrees about is that the North is enormously rich, a treasure chest that only needs unlocking. The North contains gold, silver, copper and many other metals; it also contains oil and gas, in quantities yet unmeasured but known to be huge. It had a gold rush in 1898, when easily accessible gold was found in the Klondike region of the Yukon and Dawson City's population swelled to forty thousand. Then the gold ran out, the prospectors departed, and early in this century Dawson's population fell to a few thousand. But today mining goes on all over the north, and in one recent year the Yukon yielded three hundred million dollars worth of metals, the Northwest Territories over four hundred million dollars worth. In the 1970s, as oil prices increased rapidly, the North came to be seen as the next Alberta, and oil companies invested as much as four hundred million dollars a year in northern exploration and drilling. Every year the estimates of available oil and gas increased.

These developments have brought bewildering changes to the North, and produced in the South both towering ambition and a lingering sense of guilt. Northrop Frye, the Toronto literary critic

"Inuit Igloos" is from The Polar World, 1874.

and liberal philosopher, has summed up what many Canadians feel about their use of the North: "Everywhere we look today, we see the conquest of nature by an intelligence that does not love it, that feels no part of it, that splits its own consciousness off from it and looks at it as an object." This has been the theme of much political writing about the North, and the thrust of some governments. It suggests a basic ambivalence in Canada's attitude toward the wilderness—on the one hand, we want it to be pristine in its beauty, as God left it; on the other, we are tempted by its possibilities for human and technological development.

Perhaps the best way to understand the North is to see it, so far as we can, through the eyes of the people whose home it has been for millenia. The Inuit arrived there, apparently, about five thousand years ago—they probably came from Siberia when there was a land passage across the Bering Strait, and their faces retain an oriental quality. On their time-scale, the period of contact with the white world occupies so far only a brief moment. For thousands of years they were on their own, developing a self-sufficient style of life. They lived by the natural products of the land, particularly the seal. They made their clothes from sealskin, and used seal and caribou skin to make tents and covers for their temporary houses they made from ice. They made small boats from animal skins. They ate fish, whale, sometimes bear and caribou. They formed tiny bands, some of them a few families in size, and roamed the Arctic, from what is now Alaska to Greenland, searching for food. They had a religion, based on loosely developed ideas about the creation of the world, a religion which contained sea monsters and sea goddesses and was passed on through the generations by shamans, or medicine-men. They had a moral code, based on mutual co-operation in pursuit of their society's main goal, survival. They had an art form, based on the carving of ivory tusks. (Inuit art created seven centuries before Christ has been exhibited in the great museums of the world).

A few Inuit saw white men in the sixteenth century, when European explorers began penetrating the North. Sebastian Cabot sailed to the North in search of the Northwest Passage to Asia in 1508, and there were other voyages by Martin Frobisher in 1576 and John Davis in 1585. The Inuit became aware that they were not alone in the world: each visit became part of Inuit mythology, a story told and retold over the generations until the detail was altered and elaborated. Europeans came in search of furs in the seventeenth century, and in 1780 Alexander Mackenzie of the North West Company traced the North's major river, which is named for him, down to the Arctic sea. In the late nineteenth century, white culture finally made a serious impact on the Inuit— European whalers made frequent calls in the Arctic, and they were followed by permanently established Hudson's Bay Company trading posts and Christian missionaries. In 1870 and 1880 the North came under the control of the Canadian government, and in the twentieth century the Eskimos became in effect wards of the state. At one time every Inuit was given a number by the government, to make bureaucratic handling of cases easier. The government sent in school teachers, nurses, and police. The whites traded with the Eskimos, obtaining furs (particularly, for one period, white fox furs) in return for guns and tools. The whites also brought tuberculosis and other diseases. In one way, the arrival of the whites was a blessing: a fragile way of life, in which starvation was a constant possibility and a frequent reality, was now for the first time supported by a rich government. At the same time, however, the Inuit way of life was permanently disturbed and the Inuit fell prey to new insecurities—when the market for fox fur declined, for example, the Inuit experienced a new white disease, economic recession.

Men in Ottawa now made the major decisions governing Inuit life. Hunting, which over the years had taken on a religious as well as practical significance, declined. Some Inuit went to work in the new resource industries, and many showed an aptitude for handling mechanical equipment. But as their old life disappeared they failed to adapt to white society. They became an apparently permanent under-class in the middle of the wilderness they had ruled alone for millenia—"the North is one big charity ward," as one of the most eloquent southern writers on the North has put it. In 1955 a federal minister of northern affairs declared, "The objective of Government policy is...to give the Eskimos the same rights, privileges, opportunities, and responsibilities as all other Canadians: in short, to enable them to share fully the national life of Canada." But this policy was easier to state than to execute. Today the Inuit have some of the benefits of ordinary Canadian society—aircraft make communications across the North comparatively easy, and television comes into the north via satellite. But because of transportation costs the North has the highest food prices in Canada, and Inuit rarely earn enough money to buy most of the products southern Canadians take for granted.

In only one area of life have the Inuit and the rest of Canada come together and created what is, for the moment at least, a mutually satisfactory arrangement—art. The early whalers and other whites recognized the artistic value of the objects the Inuit had carved out of ivory or stone. Often these were tiny sculptures which could be held in the hand or carried inside a garment. The Inuit had no word for "art", yet they made what to outsiders clearly seemed art objects. Often they made these things as a form of sympathetic magic—carving a tiny seal would be a way of praying that seal would appear and could be hunted. Those who made them were not set apart as artists within the community; their art was simply an extension of their life as hunters.

"Preparing Boot Soles" is from The Polar World, 1874.

In the middle of the twentieth century, the collecting of Inuit art became commonplace in the southern Canadian cities and in a few American and European centers; it was respected in the same way that the art of preliterate cultures in Africa was respected. But in the 1950s, as white influence spread through the Arctic, almost everyone who claimed to know about it believed that the art was certain to die out. Commercial pressures were corrupting it—Inuit were even being encouraged to carve ashtrays. Moreover, the life on which the art was based was disappearing.

By all the rules, Inuit art should have been destroyed. But two developments surprised everyone. One was the response of the Inuit carvers themselves. Just as their ancestors had proved adaptable to every challenge put in their way by nature, so these carvers demonstrated that they could adapt their talents to the standards of western art. Rather than declining into producers for tourist shops (though some did that), the best carvers turned into genuine artists. They put behind them the traditional anonymity of primitive artists and emerged as individualists. Soon their work began appearing in southern Canadian and American cities under the individual carvers' names. This new work, much larger in size than the carvings the whalers first saw in the nineteenth century, expressed in elaborate symbolism the nature of Inuit life and impressed collectors all over the world. It was something fresh that the artists had made from their own situation.

The second surprising development was set in motion by a southern white, James Houston. In the winter of 1957, as a federal administrator on West Baffin Island, Houston was already aware of the great value of Inuit carving. One day he was talking to a carver named Oshaweetok at Cape Dorset. Oshaweetok noticed the face of a sailor on two packages of cigarettes and remarked casually to Houston that it must be tiresome for the person who had to paint every one of those little heads exactly the same. Houston, as he began to explain that it wasn't done that way, realized there were no Inuit words for printing. He took an ivory walrus tusk Oshaweetok had recently carved, smeared it with ink, and pressed against it a piece of toilet paper. When the toilet paper was taken away it carried the design Oshaweetok had cut.

Oshaweetok looked at the result. "We could do that," he said.

Houston conceived the idea of turning the Inuit into printmakers. He learned printmaking techniques in Japan and then imported them into the Arctic. A generation later there were scores of Inuit printmakers in the Arctic, some of them organized into co-operatives that allowed them to control their lives. Their work today is known in dozens of art galleries across North America and Europe, and reproduced in scores of books. It contains the same original forms as Inuit sculpture, now flattened out on a page and brilliantly colored. The best of the Inuit prints have a dazzling energy and originality.

In recent years the fine Inuit sculptors and printmakers have been among the most prosperous and most respected artists in Canada. They find this baffling, but for the most part pleasant. Kenojuak of Cape Dorset, for example, grew up in the 1930s in what was essentially a Stone Age culture, her contact with whites limited to an occasional visit from a government ship. The great events of her childhood were migrations across the ice and successful hunts. So far as she knew, forty years ago, her life would always be limited by the Arctic horizon. Now, in her early fifties, she can look back on a career that has included trips to Rotterdam, Ottawa , Toronto, and Calgary; she has seen lavish art books devoted to her work; she has stood shyly in art galleries while collectors swarmed around her; she has seen her most famous print appear on Canadian postage stamps; her face has appeared on television and in national magazines. Kenojuak is a celebrity who has made the astonishing leap in four decades from the neolithic era to the jet age. No one will ever claim that the absorption of the Inuit into Canadian life has been an essentially happy story, but it has had its triumphant moments.

BRITISH COLUMBIA

SPLENDOR SINE OCCASU

British Columbia
Area: 948,596 sq. km.
Population: 2,744,470
Capital: Victoria

Facing page. Mount Robson, Canada's highest and best-known mountain, soars 3953 metres to the snow-capped peak. On the same mountain's eastern flank lies the other extreme of vertical terrain, Canada's deepest cave. Surveyed to a depth of over five hundred metres, Arctomys Cave is little known to any but skilled cavers, since the 2400-metre trip to the bottom is a dangerous climb. Both are within Mount Robson Provincial Park, 200,000 hectares of jagged peaks, glaciers, green lakes, white rivers, flowering valleys.

Previous page. The characteristic panorama of the Rocky Mountains, varied and magnificent, unfolds near Tête Jaune Cache. The town was named after an Indian-French guide and trapper, Pierre Hatsinaton, who stored food and furs here early in the last century. The road that runs northwest past here to the Pacific at Prince Rupert is also named after Pierre, but in the English translation: the Yellowhead Highway.

Above. The canyon of the Fraser, one of the world's most spectacular river gorges, awed even the man it was named after. "Our lives hung by a thread," wrote the explorer Simon Fraser. "We had to pass where no human being should venture." That was in 1808; well before the end of the century the CPR had laid tracks through the canyon, seen in this photograph on the right side of the river. Later the CNR built the rail line visible on the left side of the river, and later still the roadbed of the Trans-Canada Highway was cut above the CNR route.

Abandoned minesites line the trail that climbs from New Denver, on the shore of Slocan Lake, to the summit of nearby Idaho Peak. The town was first named Eldorado, renamed in the 1890s by jubilant prospectors certain their mines were richer than those at Denver, Colorado, and their town destined to become a greater city than the American one. But the ore (which here was silver, while in most of B.C.'s mountain boom towns it had been gold) ran out, alas, early in the new century, leaving the skeletons of ghost mines littering the Slocan hills.

Gold and silver lured the first wave of
newcomers to British Columbia, but the real
treasure of the region stood yet to be exploited
in the rain forest. Douglas firs, Sitka spruce, red
and yellow cedars, many of them close to a
hundred meters high, grew on ground the
Crown would lease to loggers at a cent an acre
or $6.60 a square mile. The great trees of the
climax forest have long been logged off in most
parts of the province. But the smaller logs that
are today felled by chainsaw, formed into
booms on the inlets and rivers, and moved by
tugboat to the mills, are still the source of B.C.'s
greatest riches: the multi-billion-dollar-a-year
forest industry.

Previous page. Mount Garibaldi, less than a hundred kilometres from Vancouver, commands a majestic panorama of peaks, glaciers and transparent green lakes. The mountain was named for the Italian soldier, statesman and patriot, Giuseppe Garibaldi, a choice both poetic and apt. Like the man, the mountain has a fiery disposition: as the most northerly of the Pacific Coast volcano chain that includes the presently active Mount St. Helen's, Garibaldi could erupt again.

Above. Pacific Northwest Indian designers and sculptors are often described as the most sophisticated "primitive" artists in the world. Perhaps this description betrays a dubious assumption. In what "advanced" culture have sculptors shown greater power to transmute natural forms into the symbols and shapes of plastic art? The figure of Tsonoqua, the Giantess, is by a traditional Kwakiutl carver and stands at Alert Bay, as does the Thunderbird *(right)*. The totem pole and house-front panel, *(below)*, are at Thunderbird Park in Victoria.

Facing page. After several generations of decline, the arts of the Pacific Northwest Indians have regained much of their vitality. This contemporary version of the creation myth, titled *Genesis*, is by Bill Reid. It was commissioned for permanent display at the Museum of Anthropology at U.B.C.

Greater Vancouver, Canada's third city, has a population of 1.5 million. Most of them derive their styles of living from the city's location on a mountainous seacoast. The forest of pleasure-boat masts in this photograph points to the inflatable dome of the city's new sports stadium. And from the mountain a quarter-hour distant contestants launch themselves into thin air in the annual World Hang Gliding Championship.

Facing page. Despite the encircling mountains Vancouver has a mild climate — natural ice for hockey has formed on the beaches only once in living memory, and local sportsmen speak of skiing and golfing on the same day.

Previous page. In striking contrast to the turbulent mountain gorge pictured on page 212, the Fraser River on its final hundred-kilometre passage to the Pacific Ocean has created a broad, table-flat floodplain. Dark silt carried by the river from the eroding mountains here lies 1500 metres deep. This is Canada's richest agricultural area, and perhaps its most beautiful pastoral landscape. Horse and dairy farms occupy much of the inland end of the valley; the broad delta near Vancouver grows fresh greens, fruit and flowers for the metropolis.

Below. Vancouverites speak of their city as a Pacific Rim port. By this they mean not only the grain, lumber, coal and other cargoes that move in vast quantities from here to the Orient, but also the great stream of goods and people that enter Canada from the West. Vancouver's Chinese community is Canada's oldest and largest. So at one time was the Japanese community. Dispersed by harsh fiat during World War Two, Japanese are once more settling here.

Left. Vancouver's West End, seen through the tangle of racing sails typical of a summer day on English Bay, has the densest concentration of people in Canada.

Overleaf. Lion's Gate Bridge, spanning the entrance to Vancouver's harbour, was once the world's longest suspension bridge.

Above. Orcas, the elegant black-and-white sea mammals known as killer whales, are less dangerous than their name. Among the islands of B.C.'s Inner Passage, people in kayaks often paddle right through pods of orcas without seeming to arouse the whales' curiosity, let alone their hostility.

Right. Fishing is second only to forestry as a source of wealth in B.C. The catch includes herring, here emerging from the sea in a purse seine, five kinds of salmon, and the world's greatest harvest of halibut.

Previous page. Between Vancouver Island and Alaska the open Pacific is broken by the Queen Charlottes, 150 crag-sided, densely forested islands. Only six are inhabited, mainly by Haida Indians, descendants of the people who carved the magnificent fallen totem poles that can be found at several abandoned villages.

A man-made deep water port was created at Point Roberts, south of Vancouver, by building a long finger of land across a submerged sand spit to reach the ocean channel. The principal cargo loaded here is soft coal, moved by conveyor onto huge bulk carriers.

Among Canadian cities, Victoria, the capital of B.C., has the mildest climate, the most profuse greenery, and the strongest flavour of the British colonial past. A double-decker bus will take you to a cricket match, to be followed by high tea, both on a mid-winter afternoon when most of the country lies ice-bound. The Legislative Building, which still dominates the skyline (*left*) above the harbour, preserves the exuberance of Queen Victoria's era with tiled mosaics on the floors, stained-glass in the windows, and gilded plaster on the cornices. The renowned Butchart Gardens (*above*) were created over the quarry that once supplied limestone to Robert Pim Butchart's cement plant. Today, in the Sunken Garden, the Rose Garden, the Italian Garden and the Japanese Garden, visitors take more than half a million photographs every year.

BRITISH COLUMBIA

"Indian Monuments on Canadian Pacific Coast" appeared in Scribner's Monthly, 1880.

Facing page. Long Beach, on the west coast of Vancouver Island, displays a crescent of white sand ten kilometres long facing the open Pacific Ocean. The beach is part of Pacific Rim National Park, which includes stretches of towering rain forest, over a hundred small jagged islands, and the long lava shelf that rims the margin of Canada. At high tide the shelf is submerged. At low tide this is the last step of a journey across Canada from ocean to ocean.

Most Canadians and most Europeans reach British Columbia today by air, flying high over white-tipped mountains that look from above like abstract paintings. But the most illuminating and memorable way to get there is still by the Canadian Pacific Railway. In a sense this is the ultimate Canadian experience, and to live it is to understand for a few hours the essence of the Canadian dream of empire—that dream which in the 1880s drew together all of continental Canada. You leave Calgary in the afternoon and slowly ascend through the foothills into the Rockies. Over dinner you penetrate mountain passes that astound the eye again and again with their epic grandeur. Senses exhausted, you finally sleep, and when you awake you are in the broad, open lower valley of the Fraser River, rolling toward Vancouver. The feeling now is of released tension, as if you have come out of a deep cave into the sunlight. Soon you will be in Vancouver, the third largest city in Canada and by a long way the most attrac-

"Kootenay," a wood engraving of a scene in the central highland of B.C.,
appeared in Picturesque Canada, Vol. I, 1882.

tive, with its sparkling water on three sides and its mountainous
backdrop. Your journey is the latest of many thousands stretching back to 1887, the year when the CPR's first passenger train
arrived in Vancouver and some scattered colonial fragments
began turning into a nation.

In some ways British Columbia itself remains a colony, and
British Columbians are quick to point out—often with
resentment—their dependence on distant capital, distant
markets, and the decisions of politicians in distant Ottawa, "back
East." Three decades ago the province's most distinguished journalist, Bruce Hutchison, argued that Vancouver feels less a part
of Canada than any other Canadian city: "Across all its
thoughts, like a prison wall, stands the barrier of the mountains,
cutting it off from the rest of the nation." Since then, air travel
has modified but not eliminated that mental and emotional barrier. British Columbia is still different, psychologically, from the
rest of the country, and at times the word "alienated" is not too
strong to express its feelings about the nation that lives mostly on
the other side of the mountains.

Even in climate, British Columbia is radically different. In populated southern B.C., the long, brutal winters of the Prairies and the East are unknown. The climate in British Columbia is by comparison gentle, and the heavy rainfall produces rich harvests and deep rain forests. The Canadian humorist Stephen Leacock once remarked that if he had known what B.C. was like, he would have arranged to be born there. More than other Canadians, British Columbians are devoted to gardening, sailing, skiing, the outdoor life. They are the Californians of Canada, and just as proud of their area as Californians are. In B.C. feelings of patriotism tend to focus on the province rather than on Canada as a whole and "Canadian nationalism" is viewed with skepticism. Not only those born in B.C. but people who have moved here from the East tend to see this part of Canada as uniquely beautiful. Boosterism is endemic. "Our mountains make the Swiss Alps look shabby," a famous broadcaster, Jack Webster, once typically remarked.

But if B.C. is in some ways a kind of earthly paradise, with a relaxed and comparatively amiable way of life, its residents are never allowed to forget that their prosperity is an extension of someone else's prosperity—which is the essence of economic colonialism. British Columbia is rich in timber, its forests almost unimaginably vast, but they produce jobs for British Columbians only when the United States housing industry is prosperous and wants to buy a great deal of processed wood. (In 1982, what was a recession for most of eastern Canada was a depression for British Columbia when the market for wood dried up.) British Columbia is rich in coal, too, but the new mining towns being built in the 1980s in the interior will flourish only so long as Japan wants that coal in significant amounts.

It has always been this way with British Columbia—a hinterland economy, managed from afar—and British Columbians never cease to feel their distance from the centres of power. The building of the railroad to the coast, which some important eastern Canadian politicians (including one prime minister) regarded as costly madness, was in part the fulfilment of a promise to British Columbia, made when it joined Confederation in 1871. But it was also an expression of eastern Canada's desire to exploit the riches of the Pacific Coast. In the 1880s there was competition for those riches. The confident, expansive Americans were moving deeper into their own Northwest, and American fur trappers and gold prospectors often penetrated what Canada regarded as its own. The building of the CPR to Vancouver was a way of affirming Canada's (and the British Empire's) sovereignty over this abundant territory.

The Indians had known this abundance for a very long time, of course. Living in the fjords and inlets of the coast, and on Vancouver Island (which is just off the coast and is, in area, somewhat larger than Belgium), the Indians developed a society based on plenty rather than deprivation. When Europe was experiencing the Middle Ages, these Indians were among the richest pre-literate peoples in the world. They had a ready supply of protein in the salmon-filled rivers, there was game in the woods all around them, and the climate—warmed by the great Pacific Ocean stream called the Japan Current—was neither harshly cold nor oppressively hot.

British Columbia's coast was first sighted by Sir Francis Drake, sailing north from Mexico in 1578; he claimed it for Queen Elizabeth and England, but there were to be no settlements until two centuries later. When the whites finally arrived, at first as fur traders, they understood little about the diversity of the civilization they were invading. Even today, after the work of scores of anthropologists and linguists, we have only a sketchy idea of the pre-white Indian life. Certainly it was the most elaborately organized native culture north of Mexico, a complex group of interlocking societies. In this enormous area there were probably only

"Babbine Chief" is from an 1847 oil painting by Paul Kane which is now in the
Royal Ontario Museum.

about 100,000 Indians, but in languages alone their culture must be contemplated with awe. The Vancouver writer George Woodcock has said, "There were no less than eight different linguistic groups—each as distinct from the other as Greek from Hebrew—and within these groups again there were separate tongues—often spoken only by a few hundred people—as distinct as, say, Spanish and French."

The earliest white settlers noticed that the Indians were artistically as well as linguistically inventive. Their houses, boats, baskets and eating implements were often beautifully decorated. In the forests and in the little villages on the coast, a variety of art traditions had grown up over the centuries. And when the whites arrived, these traditions flourished. If the Indians had been rich before the whites came, for a time they became richer still—and more competitive with each other. The tools brought by the whites (the steel axe, the adze, and the curved knife) quickly replaced the simpler tools the Indians had created. Now it became possible to create much more ambitious art. The art form that made West Coast Indians known around the world—the totem pole—became the dominant image, the emblem of family and tribal pride. Marius Barbeau, one of the earliest of the scholars who studied the West Coast Indians, wrote: "The benefits accruing from the fur trade at once stimulated local ambitions; they stirred up jealousies and rivalries, and incited sustained efforts for higher prestige and leadership. The overmastering desire everywhere was to outdo the others in ingenuity and wealth, power and display." The totem pole, a tree trunk carved with images of tribal history and mythology, would tower over the entrance to a house. In some towns there might be as many as thirty or forty gigantic poles, greeting the visitor in uneven rows as he approached a village on one of the rivers flowing into the Pacific.

Most of the villages for which the poles were made have long since been abandoned; most of the poles, neglected, have rotted and fallen to the ground in what has become wilderness again. Walking in the damp, lush forests near the coast, a hiker may now and then come upon a ruined, fallen pole and find a new tree growing out of it, the forest having begun the process of reclaiming the wood, turning art back into nature.

The great European anthropologist Claude Lévi-Strauss has said: "I consider that the culture of the Northwest Indians produced an art on a par with that of Greece or Egypt." That great moment in art history lasted only a few decades and then declined; nevertheless, a visitor to British Columbia today can hardly overlook Indian culture. Totem poles and related objects can be found in parks and museums (notably at the University of British Columbia's anthropology museum) and Indian styles of art turn up on everything from postcards and sweaters to murals in restaurants. The Indian culture, however, proved fragile, and since the late nineteenth century it has been in danger of disappearing entirely. While the Indians flourished in contact with the fur trade, their independent life collapsed under the weight of more extensive settlement—and their art collapsed with it. Some Indian tribes had created a unique institution, the *potlach*, a celebration which involved feasting, dancing, chanting and the giving of elaborate gifts from the host to all the guests; later the guests would be expected to reciprocate, and shamed if they failed to do so. The *potlach* baffled and alarmed the white settlers, whose civilization was focused on taking rather than giving. For much of this century the *potlach* was banned by the law, and the ban was considered a crushing blow to Indian culture. Lately the *potlach* has been revived, along with other Indian customs, and Indian art is also experiencing a revival. Some of the descendants of the great nineteenth century carvers are once more at work, stimulated by the interest of European, American, and Canadian collectors.

The first white man to chart British Columbia's coast and Vancouver Island was Captain George Vancouver, who was a crewman with Sir James Cook's expeditions in the 1770s and later returned at the head of his own. In *A Voyage of Discovery to the North Pacific Ocean and Round the World* (1798), Vancouver articulated the ambitious English colonialist's view of this kind of wilderness—"The serenity of the climate, the innumerable pleasing landscapes, and the abundant fertility that unassisted nature puts forth, requires only to be enriched by the industry of man ... to render it the most lovely country that can be imagined." In his mind he placed on those lovely shores "villages, mansions, cottages, and other buildings." Imaginatively, the colonial period was ready to begin.

Colonialism was embodied in the person of Sir James Douglas (1803–77), "the father of British Columbia." It has often been remarked in this century that British Columbia, most distant of Britain's North American colonies, is also the most British in tone—for decades Victoria, the capital of B.C. which Douglas placed at the southeast tip of Vancouver Island, was frequently referred to as the most English of Canadian cities in its style of life; and as late as 1930, a premier of British Columbia noted with pride that B.C. was "the geographic centre of the British Empire." Some of this atmosphere is owed to Douglas, who carried British formality and pomposity to lengths that suggested parody.

The child of one branch of British colonialism, Douglas lived to become the champion and dictator of another. He was born illegitimately in Demerara, British Guiana, to a Creole (partly black) woman and a Scottish businessman who had journeyed there from Glasgow in pursuit of the rum trade. Acknowledged by his father, the boy went to school in Scotland and then signed on with the North West Company and later the Hudson's Bay Company, the two fur companies that for generations functioned as the governing authorities in much of Canada. It was as a Hud-

"Man of Nootka Sound" appeared in
A Voyage to the Pacific, 1784.

son's Bay Company manager, dealing principally with the Indians in the fur trade, that Douglas crossed the Rockies into British Columbia in 1826 and began a career in which he enthusiastically combined the demands of commerce with those of government. For one period, from 1851 to 1858, he was both Chief Factor of the Hudson's Bay Company and Governor of Vancouver Island; finally, when he was made governor of the mainland colony as well, he severed his connections with the company.

Douglas was responsible for the maintenance of law and order during British Columbia's most intense period of growth, when the Fraser River gold rush of 1858 brought in thousands of American prospectors and led to the development of the interior. Douglas operated according to strict rules, learned in his Scottish school. He once remarked that in carrying out the orders of the Hudson's Bay Company, "obedience is the very first and most important of our duties, like the A.B.C. in literature." The second, apparently, was making an impression. He held to the principle by which British colonial officers of that period dressed for dinner in the jungles of Africa. In the B.C. wilderness Douglas wore lace-trimmed uniforms and laid out croquet lawns to the best British standards. As he travelled about the colony he was always lifted out of his boat or canoe by his men. He directed that guns be fired whenever he arrived at or departed from a fort: he said this was necessary to impress the Indians. A visitor from England once politely remarked that Douglas's manner had "a gravity, and a something besides which some might and do mistake for pomposity." Meanwhile, in the service of the crown he was growing privately prosperous. At one point, late in his life, he was the largest single property owner in Victoria.

Many of his fellows, particularly on the mainland, regarded him as a despot. He believed that the mainland in the 1850s had too few permanent residents to provide the basis for the sort of democracy that was slowly developing in the East. The "transients" involved in hunting, fishing, farming and mining were, in his view, incapable of ruling themselves; so he ruled them. On five occasions the citizens sent petitions over his head to the government in England, and finally the secretary of state for the colonies responded. In 1864, reluctantly, Douglas presided over the opening session of the first legislative council, and a form of democracy arrived finally on the British Columbia mainland.

Since then, government in B.C. has had a tone rather different from that in the rest of Canada. Bruce Hutchison, loyalist though he is, once wrote that "Vancouver has produced some of the worst politics in Canada." If not the worst, then perhaps some of the most extreme. Public life in British Columbia tends to be—in the political scientists' term—"polarized," often on class lines that resemble those of England. Racism has been more evident than elsewhere, directed against Asian labourers and most particularly against Japanese immigrants and Canadians of Japanese ancestry during the Second World War. In recent decades, provincial politics has been dominated by the right-wing Social Credit Party (which has usually been in power since 1952) and the left-wing New Democratic Party. Left-wing unions have played a larger role than elsewhere, and so have intransigent, union-fighting owners.

In 1903, as on many occasions since, the inept handling of labour relations in British Columbia aroused national concern, and the federal government appointed a royal commission to investigate. One of the witnesses was an enormously wealthy coal mine owner named James Dunsmuir, who had recently been premier and soon would be lieutenant-governor. Question: "Do you know of any real cause for the difficulty which the men have now in the mines?" Dunsmuir: "No I do not. The only trouble is because I won't let them belong to the union." Question: "Have you not, when you became aware of a man belonging to the union, got rid of him?" Dunsmuir: "You mean fired the heads of the union?" Question: "Yes." Dunsmuir: "Every time."

Since the outspoken Dunsmuir's time, labour relations in British Columbia have been more generously defined—labour has clear rights, and it is a long time since a capitalist admitted firing someone for organizing a union. Nevertheless, the old spirit has not entirely disappeared. On both sides, one can still detect more than a trace of the class antagonism which has made modern Britain what it is; perhaps this spirit is the last remnant of the nineteenth century colonialism which named British Columbia and settled it.

But if British Columbia is still struggling with the leftover impulses and institutions of its colonial beginnings, so in many different ways is the whole of Canada. Canadians have a past to which they are increasingly devoted, but their real task is the same one that faced the explorers who first glimpsed Canada's shores — to make something important and satisfying out of the empire to which, by great good luck, they are the heirs.